# Tying the Founding Flies



0 11557 01466 2

# Tying the Founding Flies

Mike Valla

HEADWATER
BOOKS

STACKPOLE
BOOKS

*For my wife Valerie,*
*and in memory of Walt and Winnie Dette*



Published by
STACKPOLE BOOKS
5067 Ritter Road
Mechanicsburg, PA 17055
www.stackpolebooks.com



Printed in the United States of America

10 9 8 7 6 5 4 3 2 1

First edition

Cover design by Caroline Stover
Cover image by the author
Photos by the author except where noted

**Library of Congress Cataloging-in-Publication Data**

Valla, Mike, author.
Tying the founding flies / Mike Valla. — 1st ed.
pages cm
Includes bibliographical references and index.
ISBN 978-0-8117-1466-2
1. Fly tying—United States. 2. Flies, Artificial—United States. I. Title.
SH451.V342 2013
688.7'9124—dc23

2014039057

# CONTENTS

# ACKNOWLEDGMENTS

In *The Founding Flies* (2013), I introduced a number of individuals from around the country who assisted me in obtaining valuable resources and information that made that book possible. One of the most pleasant surprises that resulted from tackling *The Founding Flies* was the friendships I made along the journey. A couple of those same individuals, now friends, assisted me with this project, *Tying the Founding Flies*.

Rick Ackel, one of André Puyans's most passionate students, invited me into his home and awesome fly-tying room in Pleasanton, California. Rick sat down with me at his tying table and offered instruction on crafting Puyans's signature patterns, the A.P. nymphs. During a recent visit I made to the Ackel home to tie flies, Rick's wife Pam made sure we had sandwiches to munch on while the two of us were busy at the tying vise. (Pam also graciously prepared a great dinner reception at her home several months before, to celebrate the release of *The Founding Flies*.) Many of Puyan's most passionate students also benefited that evening from Pam's gracious hospitality.

Dave Johnson, a skilled fly angler from Visalia, California, who assisted me with the Buz Buszek chapter in *The Founding Flies*, extended his friendship beyond that kind gesture. Dave invited me to visit Kings River, birthplace of the Kings River Caddis, one of the "founding flies" that appear in this book.

Herb Eriksson, the talented photographer who followed the streamer fly tier Lew Oatman around the Battenkill River during the 1950s, offered additional insight into Oatman and Al Prindle, "The Shushan Postmaster"—also one of the patterns selected for this book. Herb, now in his nineties, became a good friend. His lovely wife, Doris, was accommodating and helpful.

I also thank Jay Nichols and Tim Gahr at Stackpole Books for taking a hunk of marble and shaping it into a statue.

Thanks to my wife Valerie who, once again, tolerated feathers escaping from my fly-tying room, reference books piled throughout the house, and many fly-fishing road trips.

# INTRODUCTION

*"I never blame myself when I'm not hitting. I just blame the bat and if it keeps up, I change bats."*

*—Yogi Berra*

When fly anglers aren't hitting, they seldom blame themselves or their fly-fishing technique. They change flies, they change rods, they change leaders, and they even reel in and change streams. They blame the weather and they blame the water conditions—too high, too low, too clear, too cloudy, too warm, or too cold. They blame the trout, too—they're just not hitting today. They even blame chickens: their feathers aren't good enough to tie a fly that will entice fish. We need new chickens.

Our goal is to always make fish hit, even if they're not in the mood. Most often, fly tiers create new flies—there's always something different, something not yet discovered that will put the odds in our favor. So anglers return to their tying vises, time after time, and create new fly patterns. Special flies tied in this or that newfangled way, creations that will surely bring a hit. Creativity and inventiveness bloom at the tying vise. New tying materials are discovered, reported, written about, and promoted. We all want to be hitting every time we're on water.

The end result is that anglers must choose from hundreds of fly patterns. It seems that with every passing day a new fly has been "invented." The fly-tying *revolution*—more aptly labeled a *mutation*—has resulted in the death of many fly patterns that were once considered effective—flies that have brought thousands of fish to the net and much joy to the angler.

The *founding flies* are the archetypes of most every fly pattern that has followed, and they enhance our sport in special ways. Many have been lost in the sea of new fly patterns that have emerged from vises of contemporary fly tiers. Yet many archetypal patterns that have been ignored in recent times are still as effective as the day they were created. They've been given a bum rap, excused from memory, or rationalized out of existence. They've been thought of as flies that "can't hit." But, as Camden wrote in *Remaines of a Greater Worke, Concerning Britaine* (1605), "All the proof of a pudding is in the eating."

In *The Founding Flies* (2013), I examined archetypal fly patterns created many years ago. The book was an effort to bring above the radar many of the creative fly tiers who have been long forgotten or who are remembered less and less with the passing of each season. *The Founding Flies* featured 43 fly tiers who were considered progressive in their eras, whose flies were most often fished in a time now long past.

From Marbury to Marinaro, Gordon to Grant, hundreds of patterns appeared in *The Founding Flies* along with photographs of the flies, many tied by their creators. Dressings were described, but step-by-step tying instructions were not included. A book can be only so long.

*Tying the Founding Flies* fills some of that void, though my challenge was in selecting only 21 patterns out of the hundreds that appeared in *The Founding Flies*. Yet my predicament proved short-lived. I decided to open my own fly boxes, find the archetypal patterns that I still fish today, and provide step-by-step instructions for tying those flies. I also revisited memories, going back to my boyhood, when I enjoyed tying and fishing the patterns presented in these pages. Many of those experiences are sprinkled throughout this book.

For me to abandon flies such as Chauncy Lively's Carpenter Ant or Lew Oatman's Shushan Postmaster would be tantamount to deserting old friends. These are the flies that have stood by me for decades and rarely let me down. They've enabled me over many years to make the hits, to score the runs.

I didn't, of course, fish every one of the 21 patterns presented here in my early fly-fishing years. But in some cases, such as John Atherton's flies, I fished patterns close in design and coeval with his creations. In every case I tried to give the reader a sense of my own or the creators' successes with the patterns described. Each of the flies presented here was and still is an effective pattern, worthy of your tippets. My hope is to convince you that "the proof is in the pudding." The creators of these flies put a lot of thought into their designs; none were simply tying "the fly of the day."

Is my goal to create a rush back to tying and fishing *only* the founding flies, to entice you into abandoning contemporary patterns that bring you great joy and memories in the making? No, of course not. However, I'd be delighted if you went to your vise and tied the flies presented here. If you're willing to go through a learning curve, you'll find yourself "hitting well" while paying homage to the tiers who helped make our sport what it is today.

When I'm alone, on a stretch of the Battenkill River in Vermont, or hiking into a wilderness brook trout pond in the Adirondack Mountains, I sometimes have discussions with myself. Why has it all changed? Why have the old standby patterns been abandoned? Why is it that patterns that hammered fish in the past are now viewed as ineffective?

The trout haven't changed. I guess it's as Thoreau once wrote: "Things do not change; people change." Maybe the willingness to spend many hours, days, or even years learning to fly-fish has changed. Maybe expectations have changed. For me, it's always been more about the process than the actual netting of hero-fish.

That's not to say that I've been denied catching large, wild fish, or that I haven't experienced multi-fish sessions. I've netted my share over the years. Yet above all else, fishing flies that have history brings me great joy. I enjoy "fishing with ghosts," imagining what it must have been like during John Atherton's times on the Battenkill River. Now, I wade in his shadows along the same water that he once fished, casting his patterns, his "founding flies"—the Atherton series dry flies and nymphs. Two of his flies are presented in these pages.

Sometimes I crawl out of the river, talking to myself, recalling the words I read when I was a boy in William Schaldach's *Currents & Eddies*: "Singing the dirge of regret never helped anyone. I do not, therefore, mourn the loss of what once was, but from the force of circumstances can never be again. I am grateful for the memories I retain, as are the anglers who fished the Beaverkill in those days and caught not only trout but impressions and, best of all, friendships."

# CHAPTER 1

# A.P. Black Beaver

## *Nymph*

*"The reasons I first started tying a different style and series of nymphs were all based on my frustrations with the then existing patterns. Either the good nymphs were very time consuming to tie or they represented an un-lifelike blob of something on a hook, unknown in nature. Consequently, some fourteen years ago the A.P. Nymph series was started."*

—*André Puyans,*
*"Tying the A.P. Nymph Series"*
Angler, May/June 1975

Andy Puyans's former students will be quick to tell you that their mentor was all about proportions and precision tying. He had reasons for every motion, every wrap of material, and the proportions that were required to craft a well-tied fly. Nothing in his tying was done haphazardly.

If you sat down with one of Andy's students at the tying bench, to learn firsthand Puyans's tying techniques, you would hear echoes from the master's insistence on how a fly should be tied, and why. And that's exactly what happened recently when I sat down with my friend Rick Ackel, one of Andy Puyans's greatest admirers, at his tying table.

"Andy was a bit of a perfectionist," Rick explained to me during the time I was writing the André Puyans chapter in *The Founding Flies*. "He could be a bear at times but truly was a teddy bear. He was tough, but like the Dan Fogelberg song, he had 'a thundering velvet hand.'" I would have loved to be present when Andy took a razor blade to "correct" Rick's fly during a tying lesson.

Several months after that book was released, Rick invited me into his man-cave tying room at his home in California. I was there to tie the A.P. Black Beaver nymph, to learn from Rick the steps his mentor insisted upon to craft the fly.

**The A.P. Black Beaver is one of a series of A.P. nymphs André Puyans developed in the early 1960s. The A.P. nymphs are generic mayfly nymph patterns tied with natural fur bodies. The fly was the result of Puyans's frustration with existing nymph patterns, which he called "un-lifelike blobs."**

The A.P. Black is one pattern in a series that was developed by Andy Puyans in the early 1960s. Included in this series are gems such as the A.P. Hare's Ear, A.P. Muskrat Number One, A.P. Muskrat Number Two, A.P. Claret and Beaver, A.P. Beaver, A.P. Hendrickson, A.P. Peacock and Pheasant, and the A.P. Black Beaver. They are all nice-looking nymphs. A few originals, tied by Puyans, are pictured in *The Founding Flies*. They look good and they're effective. Puyans designed the patterns after his own careful observations of natural nymphs.

In designing his A.P. nymphs, Puyans concentrated on the more mobile species, the active swimmers that a fish is likely to encounter when looking for something to munch on. Andy studied the anatomical proportions of natural nymphs—lengths of tails, abdomen, thorax, and head. To Puyans, nature directed what proportions and other features were brought to the tying vise; there was nothing arbitrary in his A.P. nymph designs.

Puyans observed that nymphs have *texture* created by small anatomical gills and filaments along the abdomen, thorax, and even head. The importance of texture led Puyans to favor natural-fur dubbing. He preferred dubbing from water-loving furry animals such as beaver and muskrat to that from land-dwelling animals like rabbits.

Puyans also put more emphasis on the importance of nymph legs than on tails. Legs are robust and substantial while tails are usually fine filaments. Likewise, heads are often sizable and not overly shiny. Andy observed that nymph heads are generally the same shades as the body and thorax. Nymph wing cases are pronounced and hardy, somewhat darker than the rest of the nymph's features, especially when the nymph matures and approaches the time when it will emerge into an adult.

## Fishing the A.P. Black Beaver

Andy Puyans didn't create the A.P. Beaver nymph to represent a specific mayfly species. It's an impressionistic pattern and can be fished in a variety of settings and situations. Fly tier Ben Byng, a former Puyans student and admirer from Tracy, California, said this to me in a recent discussion:

> When fishing waters for the first time and or waiting for a hatch on known waters, I relied on the A.P. beaver because it represented a large number of mayflies. My friends and I have an on-stream quote: "When in doubt whip an A.P. out." When I returned back from my Sierra Mountain trips, Andy always had the question: "Did you fish the A.P.?" The answer was always a resounding yes!

## Tying the A.P. Black Beaver

"There are nuances in Andy's tying methods for not only the A.P. nymphs but most all of his favorite patterns," Rick Ackel explained to me when we sat down to tie the A.P. Black Beaver on a beautiful Saturday morning in California. "We should be fishing today, and not tying," I replied. But the lessons I learned that morning more than made up for what could have been a day on the water.

The first thing I learned during my tutoring session was to pay particular attention to the way the lead wire is wound on the hook; it's not arbitrary. Puyans believed that clipping off the wire on the sides of the hook shank ensures that the weight is more evenly distributed, providing a keel-like effect when the fly is submerged during fishing. It may be open to debate whether or not ending up with two half-wraps of lead wire creates a keel-like effect; however, I do think Andy's formula for determining the number of lead wire wraps is a good one, since it establishes the nymph body proportions that will follow.

Another feature of Puyans's Black Beaver is the cocked-up tail attitude. In addition to cocking up the tails with thread, the first wrap of the copper wire ribbing is directed under the tail. If you want to tie the pattern adhering to Andy's design, cock the tails up.

Also pay attention to how the stout hair legs are oriented. Don't forget the two cement points on the pattern, a technique that may be a bit different from past practice on your own patterns.

Two key materials required to tie the A.P. Black Beaver are .015-inch lead wire and small-gauge copper wire for ribbing.

## DRESSING

**Hook:** #10-18 Tiemco 3761 or Mustad 3906B
**Weight:** Lead wire (0.15 inch)
**Thread:** Black 6/0 UNI-Thread
**Tail:** Dark moose hair
**Wing Case:** Dark moose hair
**Body:** Dyed black Wapsi beaver
**Rib:** Copper wire (.006-inch)
**Legs:** Dark moose hair

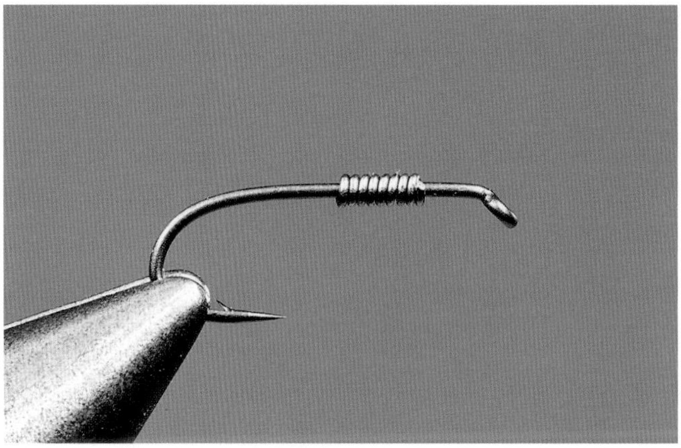

**1.** Beginning just forward of the hook shank midpoint, wind .015-gauge lead wire forward. Subtract the hook size from the number 20 to arrive at the number of lead wire wraps at both the beginning and the ending points. You'll notice on the photograph that the lead wire terminates on the *side* of the hook shank in its forward position. The same is true on the rear starting point (out of view here) with the lead wire clipped off on the side of the hook shank. Puyans believed clipping the lead wire off from the sides of the hook shank, rather than from the top and bottom of the shank, would enable the nymph to ride in the water with the wing case pointing in an upward direction.

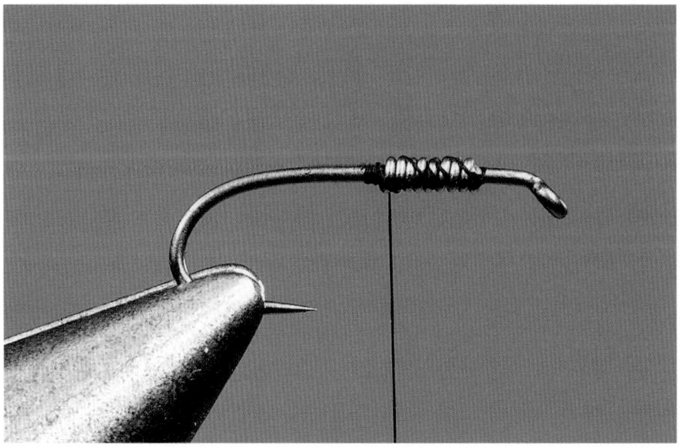

**2.** Wind thread forward through the lead wire, then return back to the rear to secure the wire onto the hook shank. This will keep all the lead wire winds from sliding backward or forward on the hook shank. The thread now rests at the rear of the lead wire wraps. Make sure that the half-wraps of lead wire don't move out of place as you're securing the lead wire to the hook shank if your intention is to follow Puyans's technique.

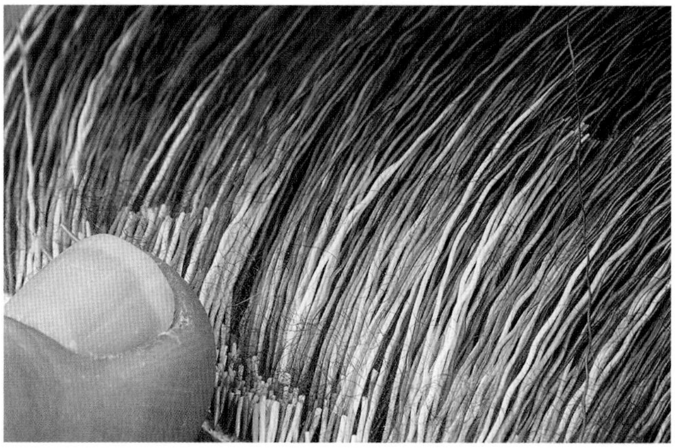

**3.** Select a tuft of moose mane hair, maybe 20 to 25 fibers for a size 10 hook as is shown here. For this pattern, you'll want the darker part of the hair, not the light-shade hair.

**4.** Stack the hair, then cut off the butt ends for more ease in handling.

**5.** Secure the tuft of hair to the hook shank. The thread now rests just in front of the hook point.

**6.** Cut off at least half of the moose hairs to form the tail. You want the bulk of the hair for the thorax wing case but only a few hairs for the tail. Spread the remaining tail-hair out.

**7.** Secure the tail to a point on the hook shank approximately above the hook barb.

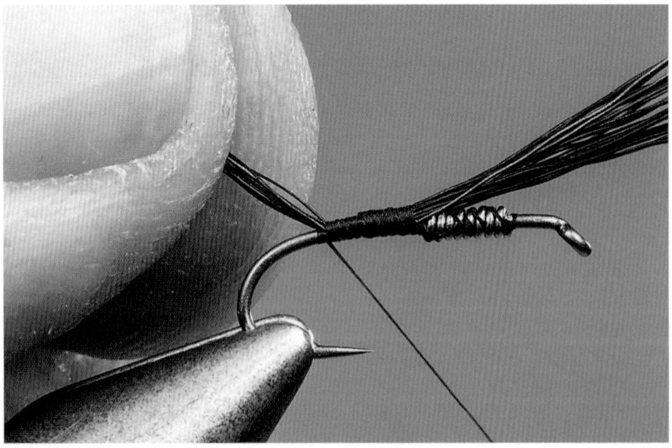

**8.** Prop up the tail by directing the thread underneath the hair fibers. Propping up the tail is an important feature of the A.P. nymphs.

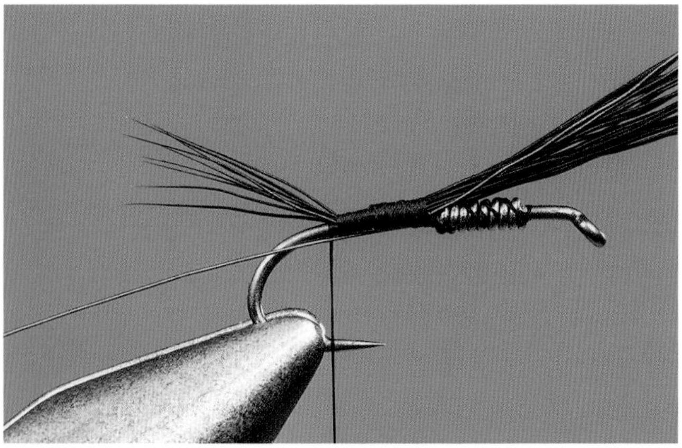

**9.** Secure a copper wire in the lower quadrant at the tail position as shown.

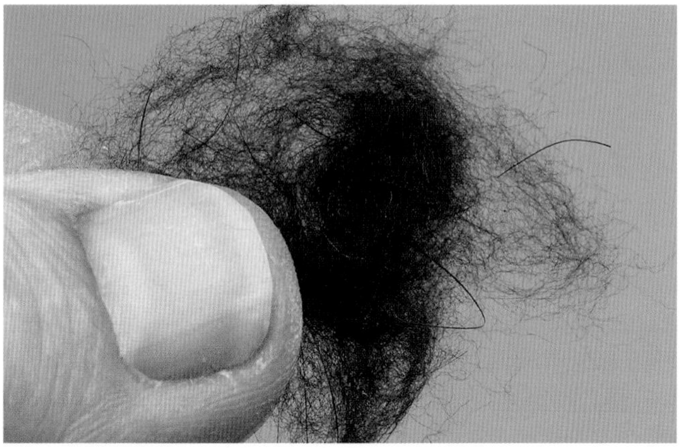

**10.** Select a small quantity of black beaver dubbing.

**11.** Attach dubbing to thread by rolling it with fingers counterclockwise.

**12.** Wind the dubbing forward. Lift up and pull back the moose mane hairs to get them out of the way. End with one wrap of the body material in front of the moose hair. The thread rests in this position, waiting to accept the copper wire ribbing.

**13.** Your first turn of the copper wire is directed underneath the tail fibers. This helps maintain the tail's cocked-up position. Continue the winds up through the lead wire. Break or snip off the copper wire once the wraps are completed.

**14.** Make sure that the beaver-dubbing body is somewhat fuzzy. Puyans made a point that the fuzziness simulates tiny nymph gills. If you find that your body material isn't fuzzy enough, you can gently rub the dubbing with a small piece of Velcro, either before or after the body is ribbed with the copper wire. There are two cement points on the nymph. The first one is here. Add a small amount of head cement to the lead wire.

**15.** If you've run out of beaver dubbing on your thread, add an additional quantity to build up the thorax into roughly a football shape.

**16.** Grasp the moose hairs that remain forward of the point where some were clipped away to form the fly tail. With your thumb and index finger, pull forward to form the tightly compacted wing case.

**17.** Secure the wing case hairs with a couple wraps of thread. Make sure you don't crowd the area just behind the hook eye. Separate out three hairs on each side of the hook; these will serve as the nymph legs. The leg hairs should be directed to the rear along the sides of the thorax.

**18.** Clip the remaining excess of moose hair that is hanging off the front of the fly. Be careful not to inadvertently snip your tying thread.

**19.** Add a drop of head cement. You have to add it at this juncture since you won't want to add it after the small beaver-fur head is created, or else it will wick up into the fur.

**20.** Add what Puyans instructed as a "skosh" of dubbing to the tying thread. You don't want much on the thread or else you might over-skosh it. Puyans defined a skosh as a third of what you might think a skosh is—very little.

**21.** Make a couple winds with your skosh of dubbing to form the head. In my example here, I've *slightly* over-skoshed the head, just as Puyans warned could happen. (I should have paid more attention to admonitions). Throw a whip-finish knot to secure the head.

**22.** Gather the six nymph hair legs, three on each side projecting to the rear, and clip off just behind the wing case.

**23.** The completed A.P. Black, still an effective fish-getter on most any water.

CHAPTER 2

# Atherton Number One

## *Dry fly*

*"The flies used for so discriminating a fish as the trout should, first of all, have the appearance of life."*

*—John Atherton,*
The Fly and the Fish, *1951*

John Atherton, a talented illustrator and contemporary of Norman Rockwell, developed his Atherton dry fly series on his beloved Battenkill River in Arlington, Vermont, where, beginning in the 1940s, he lived and maintained his studio. Atherton described his series, simply named Number One through Number Seven, as representing color gradations from light to dark. The Number One is the lightest shade in Atherton's series.

In *The Founding Flies*, I describe in great detail Atherton's fly design theories and their link with the tenets practiced by the nineteenth-century impressionistic school of artists. In short, Atherton brought the ideas of impressionistic artists, such as Monet and Renoir, to his fly-tying vise.

In his classic *The Fly and the Fish*, Atherton observed that a live insect such as a mayfly, one that a fly tier is attempting to imitate with an artificial trout fly, possesses coloring that is "impressionistic." Magnified, an insect's shade is composed of many tiny differences in tone. Variations in color, texture, and light reflections combine in living things to project "the appearance of life." Insects display a kaleidoscope of tones and shades. To best recreate the colors of their surroundings, the impressionistic artists studied how the natural world reflected or absorbed light. Atherton employed such impressionistic practices in selecting materials to craft his trout fly patterns.

**Atherton Number One dry fly, the lightest in John Atherton's dry-fly series, has the "speckled look" that he preferred in all of his patterns. The buggy look of the Atherton Number One provides features that exhibit "the appearance of life."**

Battenkill River, Arlington, Vermont. Atherton's home was near the banks of the Battenkill River, a stream inhabited by trout "gifted with a degree of caution rarely encountered in the breed." The Battenkill was the laboratory that inspired him to develop a series of dry flies that would better his chances of netting its hyperselective brown trout.

## Fishing the Atherton Number One

If you've experienced success with the buggy, classic Adams dry fly—a dark pattern—you'll also want to try this classic. It's a great fish taker on any water, and is especially useful during evening fishing; it's easy to spot floating along on a riffle in the last light. You might also have some fun with the pattern fishing it during a mayfly emergence, when the natural's color shade best matches the Atherton Number One dry fly. I enjoy fishing the Atherton Number One as a searching pattern, a fly not intended to represent any specific natural insect.

During on-stream situations when fish are not surface feeding, the Atherton Number One floating through choppy water can sometimes stir some interest from trout. The pattern is good in small hook sizes—down to size 16—during late-season fishing on small brooks. There's nothing more pleasurable than casting a small Atherton Number One off a 7-foot, 4-weight rod upstream into a small pool or riffle on a tiny trout-filled brook, especially in the fall season.

## Tying the Atherton Number One

Wing material selection did not escape Atherton's scrutiny. Most of the Atherton series dry flies, which were presented in *The Founding Flies*, used wood-duck flank feathers; he liked the "specked look" of that feather because it comported more readily with impressionistic theories than did the heavy, thick, opaque featherwings common on dry flies in his era. An exception is the wing material he used on the Atherton Number One, the pattern we're tying here.

Atherton noted that "hackle points are probably the closest thing to the natural fly wing in appearance, and I have found them effective for certain patterns." He also wrote, "There is nothing quite as good for imitating the very light, pale duns. The natural dun hackle point is amazingly lifelike." The pattern, in particular, that Atherton was referring to was the Number One.

The Number One also uses the sparkling characteristics of oval gold tinsel, a material Atherton used on most all his dry flies. "It suggests the shimmer of the insect," he wrote. Light reflection in Atherton's Number One, through the use of gold tinsel, held true to impressionism axioms.

Atherton's hackle selection for the pattern also adhered to impressionistic principles. He used cree, which exhibits multishades of brown, ginger, tan, black, and cream. Even today, in the era of genetic hackle, cree capes are difficult to obtain. Atherton used cree but recognized that it was sometimes necessary to mix a grizzly hackle with another shade, such as ginger, to approximate the "mixed shade effect" of cree. His alternative hackle for the Number One was a mixture of pale ginger and grizzly, two common shades.

The mixture of hackle shades contributes to the fly's "buggy" appearance, which in turn no doubt contributes to its effectiveness. It exhibits the "appearance of life," as Atherton embraced, and also the the quality of "insectness" that fly angler Ted Trueblood believed was so important in trout fly design. And then there's the buggiest of all fly-tying body materials—hare's ear. Atherton wrote, "The little spotted hairs combine with the softer pinkish hair at the base of the ear to make a wonderfully lifelike effect." For Atherton, "appearance of life" in trout fly design was the *sine qua non*.

## DRESSING

| | |
|---|---|
| **Hook:** | #12-16 Mustad 94840 |
| **Thread:** | Tan UNI-Thread |
| **Wing:** | Light, glassy dun rooster hackle points |
| **Tail:** | Light dun hackle barbs |
| **Rib:** | Lagartun oval gold tinsel (small or medium) |
| **Body:** | Pale cream fox fur |
| **Hackle:** | Light cree, or light ginger and grizzly mixed |

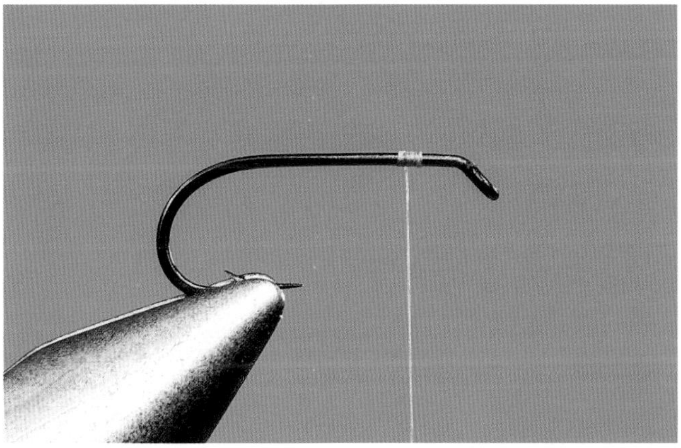

**1.** Begin thread on hook shank set back from the eye ⅛ inch to $^3/_{16}$ inch (depending on the hook size). In this example, we're going to finish the fly with a small, clean space behind the hook eye traditionally used for a turle knot leader attachment. (Leaving a turle knot space is just my preference when tying most dry flies; it's the Catskill style. The wings will be set back from the hook eye a little more than you might be accustomed to.) You can also use the two-thirds point on the hook shank as the thread starting point.

**2.** Select two light, glassy natural dun rooster hackles, the points of which will be used for wings. Select hackles that have points as broad or rounded as possible—which is sometimes a challenge with genetic hackle. But you're going to want to use rooster (if possible) rather than hen hackle tips; hen hackle is not as glassy as rooster hackle.

**3.** Place the convex sides (shiny sides) of the hackles against each other so that, once tied on the hook shank, the wings will diverge. It's best not to cut out the hackle points from the entire feathers when attaching to the hook. You'll trim the long feather stem back in the next step. John Atherton advised not to strip the barb fibers totally away from the quill in tying the feathers onto the hook shank. Some barbs should be left on the stem to reinforce the center quill, which tends to be weak. Hackle point wings can be fragile, and they need strength at their attachment points on the hook. Some barb fibers will flare out in the process of tying in, but you can trim the strays away.

**4.** Cut off the excess hackle stems that served to allow easier manipulation of the wings while attaching to the hook shank.

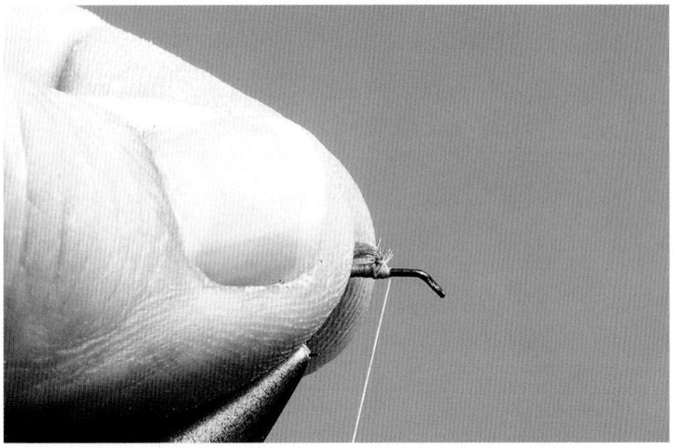

**5.** Encircle the bases of the hackle points with thread and then make a couple more thread wraps behind the wing. Add additional wraps in front of the wing, which will dam up the wing into an upright position. You can trim away any stray hackle barbs that may be jutting out of position.

**6.** Make a couple more thread wraps around the wing bases to position the wings. Also run the thread between the wings—rear to front and then front to rear—to separate the wing points. Turn the vise jaw so that you can view straight between the wings you've set to make sure they are centered directly on top of the hook shank and not leaning to the side. You can carefully reposition the wings with your fingers if necessary.

**7.** Select dun hackles that have long, stiff barbs for tailing. It's sometimes difficult to find hackle with long barbs on genetic hackle capes, but do the best that you can. Tie in the hackle barbs at a point on the shank above the hook point. Try to select barbs that are at least as long as the hook shank (I like my tails a tad longer).

**8.** Trim the butt ends of tailing barbs. Attach and secure a length of Lagartun oval gold tinsel (medium or small size depending on hook size) at the point where the tailing departs the hook shank.

**9.** Spin cream-shade fox fur dubbing onto the tying thread, using your method of choice.

**10.** Wrap dubbing forward to a point just short of the wings, then secure with two wraps of thread. Once the body dubbing is in place, begin even wraps of the tinsel forward to just short of the wings.

**11.** Snip excess tinsel, being careful not to inadvertently cut the tying thread.

**12.** Atherton recommended light cree hackle for this pattern but also suggested, as an alternative, wrapping a mixture of grizzly and light ginger hackle. Recognizing that cree hackle capes are sometimes difficult to acquire, the substitute hackle is shown here, since grizzly and light ginger are readily available. Combining the two hackle shades will result in the mixed-shade effect Atherton preferred in his patterns. Tie in as shown. The hackle size selected is twice the hook gap, a little longer than the length preferred by many contemporary fly tiers.

**13.** Snip the excess hackle quill butts, and make sure the feather stems are secured in position. Grasp the grizzly hackle with hackle pliers and begin wrapping forward.

**14.** Make two or three turns of grizzly hackle behind the wings, then two turns in front of the wings. Be certain not to crowd the hook eye. Tie off. Note the longer than usual hackle barb lengths, typical of Atherton and Catskill-style dry flies.

**15.** Grasp the light ginger hackle then wrap it forward through the grizzly hackle. Use a slight weaving, back-and-forth motion as you wrap the ginger forward. The weaving will lessen the chance of matting down the grizzly hackle during wrapping. Secure the ginger hackle just short of the hook eye with a couple thread wraps. (If you've found that the hackle has encroached the hook eye, straddle the hook shank with your thumbnail and middle digit nail then shove the hackle back a bit.) Snip off the excess hackle, being careful not to cut the tying thread.

**16.** Tie off the head with a whip-finish knot. As mentioned at the beginning of the tying sequence, we're tying this dry fly maintaining a small, clean hook shank space behind the hook eye. This space is used for a traditional turle knot leader attachment. Some of the classic Catskill-style fly tiers who crafted Atherton dry flies left a turle space. (Maintaining the small, clean space is just my preference for this fly, given my Catskill tying upbringing, but it is not a requirement by any means. Most tiers prefer a full head.)

**17.** Add a drop of head cement.

**18.** The Atherton Number One dry-fly, completed, with its mix of hackle shades.

# CHAPTER 3

# Atherton Number Two

## *Nymph*

*"When a hatch appears, the short period before the emergence of the duns can be fished best with a close imitation of the natural nymph, although even at that time the impressionistic nymph of the general type is often successful."*

—*John Atherton,* The Fly and the Fish, *1951*

As with his dry flies, Atherton insisted on employing the principles of the impressionistic school of artists to his nymph patterns. And like his dry-fly series, Atherton named his nymph patterns Numbers One to Three. These three patterns, along with other details concerning John Atherton and his flies, were presented in *The Founding Flies*. The Number One nymph, as is true with his Atherton Number One dry fly, was his lightest shade pattern. The Number Two was a medium shade, and the Number Three was the darkest of the three nymphs. Atherton designed the patterns with impressionistic tenets as well as practicality in mind. The Atherton Number Two nymph is simple in its design and is also easy to tie. It's essentially a hare's ear nymph with a bright blue wing case.

Given the simple design, a fly tier can pump out hundreds of Number Two nymphs with some of the least expensive tying materials available. There's no tragedy in losing lots of them while casting in precarious fish-holding areas on your favorite stream. The Number Two's simplicity was born out of Atherton's fishing experiences on his home waters—the Battenkill; he himself lost a lot of nymphs while casting them in difficult spots. As the well-known Battenkill fly angler and fly-fishing writer John Merwin wrote in his book *The Battenkill* (1993), the river has a relatively

**The Atherton Number Two nymph exhibits rough texture created by hare's ear fur. The random fur guard hairs projecting out along the abdomen provide a lifelike effect, simulating natural nymph gills. The sparkle of oval gold tinsel suggests the shimmer found in naturals.**

Ithaca Falls, near the Cornell University campus, is the final plunge Fall Creek makes on its journey to Cayuga Lake, a couple of miles downstream in Ithaca, New York. Nice-size rainbows frequent the stream in this section during their early spring spawning runs. Landlocked salmon and brown trout run the creek in the fall, offering fly anglers late-season sport. Hare's ear nymphs proved effective along that Fall Creek stretch. Fish often held in the Slot, best fished by standing on the narrow cliff edge above the current.

The Atherton Number Two nymph is an effective pattern for all trout species. Brook trout love the buggy look and the gold tinsel flash. This one was caught on John Atherton's home river, the Battenkill.

low gradient of slow-flowing pools and brief riffles. Many trout hang close to the banks since there's not a lot of mid-stream habitat and cover.

Wild, stream-bred Battenkill trout—the river in Vermont is not stocked—need cover for safety (many trout-hungry Merganser ducks call the Battenkill their home). As Atherton discovered, the trout tend to hang close to the river banks, especially where there's overhanging brush and sunken debris.

"When fishing with the nymph," Atherton wrote, "I find it exceedingly difficult to keep my boxes well-stocked, as my losses exceed production. As so many of my best brown trout are taken by casting the nymph very close to the bank and under overhanging branches, I discover frequently that the risks necessary to the proper presentation result in many flies hung up and never recovered."

I'm featuring the Number Two because long-shanked hare's ear nymphs of a similar style have a long history in my own fly boxes, going back to my college years some four decades ago. Hare's ear as a material in trout flies goes back centuries; T. C. Hofland, in his *British Angler's Manual* (1839), made several references to the material. Hare's ear nymph patterns have always been my favorites; I fished them often as far back as the mid-1970s on both Cascadilla Creek and Fall Creek in Ithaca, New York.

A couple of years ago, a fly angler approached me at one of the national fly-fishing gatherings and asked, "Say, aren't you the guy who used to fish big hare's ear nymphs down at Fall Creek, just down the road from the campus?" I had to think twice about his question but responded, "Yes, I'm the guy!" The nymph he remembered was essentially an Atherton Number Two, without the wing case. In those early years, I routinely fished the long-shanked hare's ear nymph pattern along with a few hare's ear wet flies.

Jeff Kurt, an engineering student back in the mid-'70s, also fished Fall Creek below Fall Creek Falls, whenever he could, sometimes during lunchtime. I remember us cutting quite a few classes (at least I did) and heading down to what we called "the Slot" on Fall Creek, a holding lie for big Cayuga lake-run landlocked salmon and a few rainbow trout. To reach the Slot, we had to walk—if you can call it that—along a foot-wide rocky ledge above rushing water several feet below. When we run into each other now at the fly-show events, we both laugh about our fishing balancing act. His remembrances of those days when I bragged about the effectiveness of hare's ear nymphs brought us back together.

A hare's ear nymph, similar to Atherton's pattern, was also responsible for my netting one of the most gorgeous wild brown trout I've ever landed, on nearby Cascadilla Creek. It's a tiny brook really, something the size of a small ditch in its upper reaches. A population of wild brown trout once inhabited the small, brushy stream during my college years. It was rare to see anyone else fishing the little brook; it was more convenient to campus than it was enticing.

I remember riding a bike to its upper reaches, just after final exams were over in May. Casting the nymph into a small pool near a bank-side log, a 12-inch wild brown hammered it. It was a gorgeous fish and I've relished the memory of that day and that trout, a beauty taken on a large hare's ear nymph.

## Fishing Atherton Number Two

The small amount of lead wire attached to the hook shank usually provides ample weight to get the nymph in front of a fish's nose or get the fish's attention, depending, of course, on the water type you're fishing and the season. I've fished similar hare's ear nymphs without any weight, relying instead on a heavy-wire hook to get the fly submerged. In some instances and situations, I've found that hare's ear nymphs such as the Number Two—especially in small sizes—will take fish just under the water surface as an emerger pattern; weight is not always required to get a fish to notice that your fly might provide a tasty food morsel. Atherton's Number Two nymph is a versatile pattern.

It's a good pattern for brown trout and rainbow trout in both small brooks and larger rivers. Brook trout love the fly's buggy look as well as the tinsel's gold flash.

## Tying the Atherton Number Two

The Atherton Number Two nymph is an easy fly to tie. The primary material, hare's ear, is readily available and inexpensive. The only material that may have you scratching your head is the bright blue kingfisher feather that's required for the wing case. Kingfisher is readily available and not overly expensive. However, even Atherton himself experimented with substitute materials. If you decide to use the "bright blue feather from wing of English kingfisher" Atherton recommended for the wing case, you may experience some frustrations.

It's unclear whether Atherton used small wing-feather quill slips or the small covert feathers for the wing case that sits over nymph's thorax. In either case, if you're tying anything but small-size nymphs you'll soon discover that the covert feathers, or feather quill slips, are not large enough to create the wing case. The wing quill feathers are quite small and narrow

Kingfisher feathers are fragile, a characteristic that Atherton himself recognized. Another problem is that it's difficult to maintain the striking blue shade once the feather or feather slip is folded forward over the thorax in creating the wing case. The backs of the blue feathers are drab gray; when the feather is folded, the gray sides of the fibers tend to turn and rotate and mix in with the blue.

Many tiers in the past have used blue floss folded over the thorax, as recommended by Atherton as a substitute material, to create the bright blue wing case. Harry and Elsie Darbee, Catskill-region fly tiers that Atherton mentioned in his book as a source for all the patterns he featured, used blue floss for wing case material. The wing case shade is probably more important than using kingfisher feathers, although once floss becomes submerged in water, it loses its color. However, in the tying procedure here, I decided to use the real thing.

You'll also want to make sure that the hare's ear body is scruffy-looking once it's completed. That adds to the attractiveness of the pattern—at least from a trout's perspective. Complete hare's ears and masks are inexpensive; preparing your own hare's ear fur mix will ensure that you'll have dubbing full of the small, tiny guard hairs that make the material scraggly and buggy looking.

### DRESSING

| | |
|---|---|
| **Hook:** | #8-14 Mustad 9671 |
| **Weight:** | Lead wire (.015-inch) |
| **Thread:** | Black UNI-Thread |
| **Tail:** | Ring-necked pheasant tail feathers, three fibers |
| **Rib:** | Lagartun oval gold tinsel (small or medium) |
| **Body:** | Hare's ear tied rough and picked out |
| **Wing Case:** | Bright blue kingfisher or blue floss |
| **Hackle:** | Gray or brown speckled partridge |

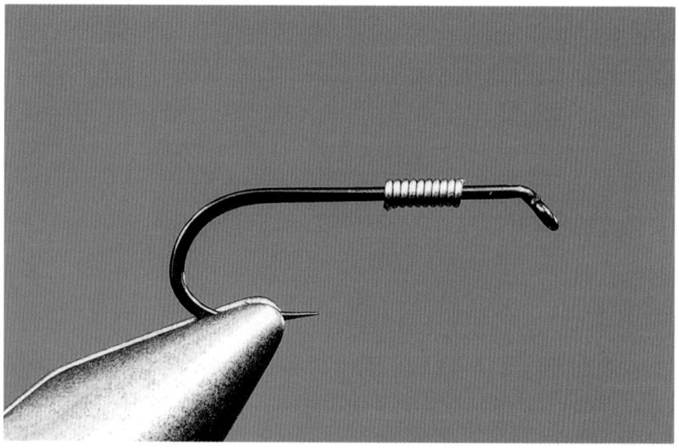

**1.** Wrap several turns of .015-inch lead wire at the middle of the hook shank. A good consistent method to determine how many turns is to subtract the hook size from the number 20 (Andy Puyans used this method for all of his his A.P series nymphs).

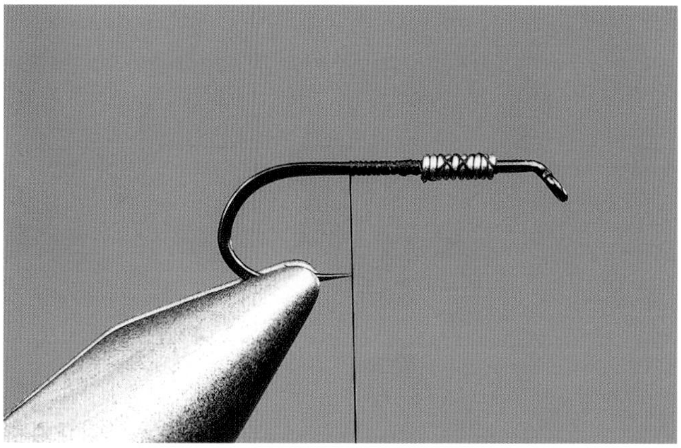

**2.** Start tying thread at the rear of the lead wire wraps. Wrap thread over the lead wire to the front, then return to the rear. The thread will rest on the hook shank almost directly above the hook point.

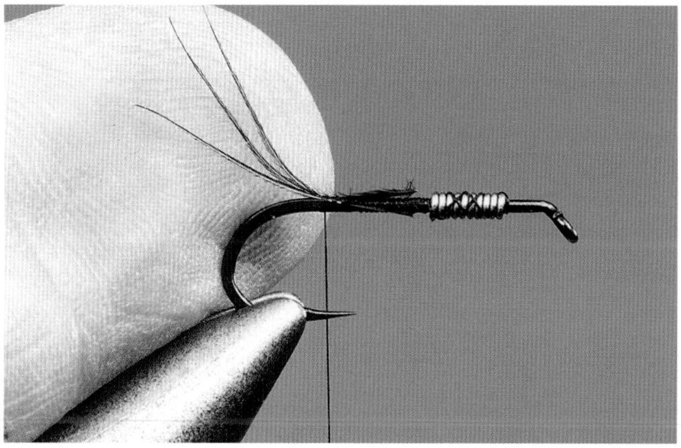

**3.** Secure three ring-necked pheasant tail fibers at the point directly above the hook point. The approximate length of the fibers is three-quarters of the hook shank length. Wrap thread toward the hook bend, ending at a point approximately above the hook barb. Secure a length of either medium or small Lagartun brand oval gold tinsel, depending on hook size.

**4.** Prepare a mix of hare's ear dubbing. You want lots of hairs mixed in with the smooth fur as this Atherton nymph relies on a ragged texture to simulate insect gills.

**5.** With the tinsel attached to the hook shank, spin hare's ear dubbing onto thread.

**6.** Wrap the body dubbing up to or slightly beyond the rear extent of the lead wire.

**7.** Wrap the oval gold tinsel through the hare's ear, ending at the forward extent of the body.

**8.** Kingfisher, rather than blue floss, is used in this example to form the wing case. As you can see in this photo, kingfisher wing feathers are bright blue.

**9.** Whether you decide to use a kingfisher feather or floss, tie in the material at the forward extent of the body dubbing. If you use a kingfisher feather, tie it in with the quill pointing to the hook rear, as shown.

**10.** After tying in the wing case material, add some additional hare's ear dubbing to the thread. You'll wrap thread over the protruding feather or floss ends lying on the lead wire, or simply snip off the excess with scissors.

**11.** Create the nymph thorax by winding the dubbing over the lead wire. Add enough dubbing to create a beefier thorax than the narrower abdomen. Make sure that you leave adequate space behind the hook eye to accommodate the partridge hackle that will be wrapped next.

**12.** Gently pull the feather (or blue floss) over the top of the thorax tightly, then secure with two wraps of thread.

**13.** Snip off the excess kingfisher feather, or blue floss, then tie in a small gray or brown speckled partridge hackle feather.

**14.** Grasp the end of the hackle feather with hackle pliers, then wrap it to a point just short of the hook eye, being careful to not crowd the eye. The feather is fragile; take caution during winding to avoid having it break off.

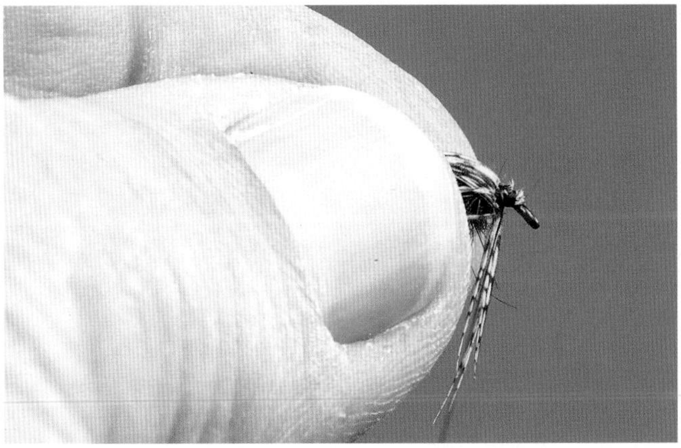

**15.** After securing the hackle with two thread wraps, gently stroke back the feather fibers so that they will be directed to the rear. Once you have them secured with thumb and index finger into rear-pointing direction, wrap turns of thread over the fibers.

**16.** Secure with a whip-finish knot and add a drop of head cement.

**17.** The completed Atherton Number Two nymph.

Oriskany Creek, a lovely farm-country stream in central New York, gave up many wild brown trout to anglers fishing the founding flies. Among the flies still effective today are hare's ear nymphs, along with terrestrials such as the Carpenter Ant.

CHAPTER 4

# Carpenter Ant

## *Dry fly terrestrial*

*"I dropped my Carpenter Ant lightly in the path of the cruising trout. He took it with such unhurried softness that I almost missed him. By the time Marion arrived I had taken and released nine browns from eleven to fifteen inches—and I hadn't covered half the pool."*

—*Chauncy K. Lively, "The Carpenter Ant," 1964* Fisherman's Digest

My first encounter with Lively's Carpenter Ant occurred some forty-five years ago, and the fly has been part of my late-season fly box arsenal ever since. Despite all of the contemporary ant patterns that have come into existence—and there are loads of them—the folded deer-hair Carpenter Ant is the only black ant pattern I've ever fished, and will ever fish. I have that much confidence in the fly.

To end my association with the Carpenter Ant, in favor of a fashionable foam-tied creation, would be tantamount to abandoning an old friend. The pattern has been a companion who has never let me down, a workmate who has come to my rescue on many occasions during the dog days of summer when netting trout seemed almost hopeless. I have so many memories of fishing the pattern as a boy, of the joy I got from the success I had with it, that it would be impossible for me to ever let the Carpenter Ant retire. I'm too attached to it.

In *The Founding Flies* I wrote about the circumstances surrounding my love affair with the pattern. In 1969 or 1970, my cousin Dave and I were wandering around my hometown—Binghamton, New York—searching for old fishing magazines and books at various bookstores and shops. During my teenage years, fly-fishing trade magazines were nonexistent; there never seemed

**Chauncy Lively's Carpenter Ant is one of the most effective terrestrial ant patterns ever developed. Lively used it with great success for both bass and hypercritical brown trout found in many Pennsylvania streams.**

Carpenter Ant took this nice Oriskany Creek brown trout during a recent trip to the small, central New York stream. The ant performed well for me that day, just as it did in the same stream sections I fished as a boy many years ago. It's an old friend that has never disappointed me.

to be enough fly-fishing stories on the magazine racks to satisfy my growing enthusiasm for the sport. Dave spotted a used copy of the 1964 *Fisherman's Digest*. I read it cover to cover, and Lively's story about his Carpenter Ant blew me away. A few days later, I was tying dozens of the pattern, in many sizes, and ordering black-dyed deer body hair in bulk from Herter's fly-tying supply house. I corresponded with Lively, telling him how his article in the *Digest* inspired me to tie and fish his creation. He returned a letter indicating he still fished the pattern with great success; it still performed for him just as well as it had one of the first times he fished it, on Pennsylvania's Young Womans Creek during dismal low-water, August conditions.

My own first success with the fly occurred on Oriskany Creek, a small stream in central New York State during the same summer I first tied the pattern. I remember that the little creek was a bit off-color from a recent rain but still wadeable, even with the hip boots that I wore in those years.

There was a small, slow-moving pool tucked back in the woods, its bank lined with brush. I remember that I cast the Carpenter Ant well upstream, almost out of boredom by that point in the day. The fishing was slow; I hadn't netted anything that entire morning. Then suddenly, I felt a slight tug on my line and a fish was on. It happened just as Lively described in his own story. The small, 7- or 8-inch trout just sucked it in "with such unhurried softness."

That small brown trout was more than enough to increase my enthusiasm for the pattern. The Carpenter Ant proved effective during late-summer trout fishing not only on the Oriskany but on other streams as well. From that point forward, I tied hundreds of the Carpenter Ants—in sizes from 12 down to 18—maybe even down to 20. Soon thereafter my fly fishing vest was overloaded with Carpenter Ants. A huge plastic bin box, chock full of ants, occupied the entire back pouch space of my vest. If I came across another fly fisher during subsequent trips to Oriskany or other streams, the big box came out and a few ants were dropped into waiting hands. I was that fond of the pattern, and that eager to share it with others.

Forty years after netting my first Oriskany brown trout on the ant, I returned to the stream to see how it would still perform—or to determine if it would perform to the degree that it once did. My return to the Oriskany, fishing the ant, is described in the July/August 2011 issue of *Eastern Fly Fishing* magazine, in a feature titled "Highway 20 Corridor, NY: Beating the Heat in Summer."

It was a beautiful summer day when I arrived at the Oriskany early in the morning. My first stop was the Chenango Canal tributary, just above the little dam that spills water into the creek. The canal at the junction with the Oriskany is deceptive, not even crotch-deep in the summer, and narrow. Unlike the Oriskany, where riffles and pools flow over rubble, stone, and rock substrate, the Chenango Canal is smooth and clear and seemingly motionless, bordered by brushy banks and rife with aquatic vegetation; this is Carpenter Ant water at its best.

Hanging tight to the right bank, I looped out 25 feet or so of DT 3-weight line along the brush on the opposite bank, with 12 feet of leader and 7X tippet dangling a Carpenter Ant. The ant dropped to the motionless water, causing a small wake. A beautiful foot-long brown trout sipped it in. After taking a half-dozen trout, I reeled in and headed downstream to the Oriskany itself.

Standing on the Oriskany's stream bank that day wiped away the intervening years and brought back memories of adventures fishing the creek as a teenager. There was the time in 1971 that I asked my high school friend Tommy Malenich to talk his father into driving us to the stream so we could fish Carpenter Ants. On that hot, late summer day I caught one of the most beautiful, deeply colored brown trout I've ever netted. He fell for my Carpenter Ant. I remembered that day on the stream with Tom, his father, and his uncle Mick with clarity but I was unable to find the exact location where I first caught an Oriskany brown trout on the ant—a lot had changed. However, I was able to locate a place on the little creek where, I remembered, a natural cold spring poured in.

After gazing down into the water from my vantage point along a road, I could see a few fish darting around. I decided to fish the pool after a lunch break with my wife, Valerie, who came along on the trip. However, she suggested that I fish now and eat later, so I soon found myself down in the water, below a logjam, casting my ant. Within seconds—maybe on the second cast—a big brown pounded the fly. I yelled to Valerie, who was waiting on the road above the stream, to bring down

Chenango Canal, a tributary of Oriskany Creek, is prime Carpenter Ant water. Stealth is the word on the Chenango Canal when casting Carpenter Ants along the overhanging brush. It's a fabulous stream to fish, even in late summer.

the camera. It wasn't the first time Valerie's nudging led to a netted fish. And that one was a nice, wild, 14-inch Oriskany brown trout.

## Fishing the Carpenter Ant

It didn't take me long to figure out the best way to fish the Carpenter Ant. It's a late-season terrestrial pattern that's best fished in slow-moving water, casting upstream next to deadfalls and along the stream bank especially near overhanging brush. You want the falling ant to create a small wake when it plops on the water surface. The small disturbance caused by the ant attracts a fish's attention in a hurry.

## Tying the Carpenter Ant

The Carpenter Ant is an easy fly to tie, about as simple as it gets. All you need is a dry-fly hook, tying thread, and dyed black deer body hair. Beginners and seasoned tiers alike can master the technique in minutes. While deer hair is fragile, it's also inexpensive. You can tie hundreds of Carpenter Ants for just a few dollars.

Chauncy Lively wrote that the ant's only drawback is its poor durability. Trout teeth are sharp and can sever the hairs. But just as Lively described, all you have to do is trim away any broken hairs after netting a fish. While the ant may start to appear disheveled, it will continue to take fish.

## DRESSING

**Hook:** #10-18 Mustad 94840
**Thread:** Black 6/0 UNI-Thread
**Body:** Black deer body hair

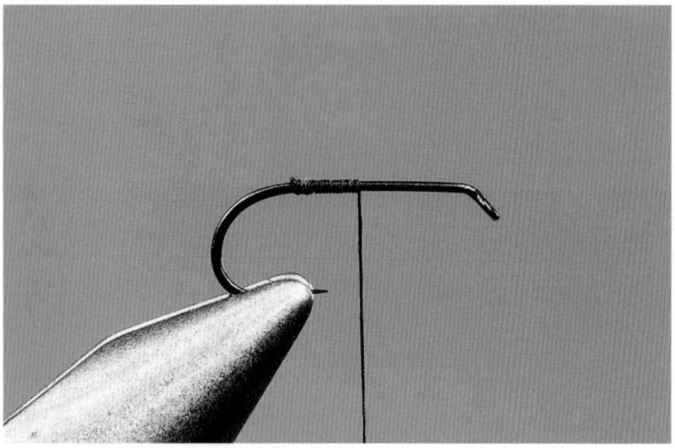

**1.** Attach tying thread at hook midpoint.

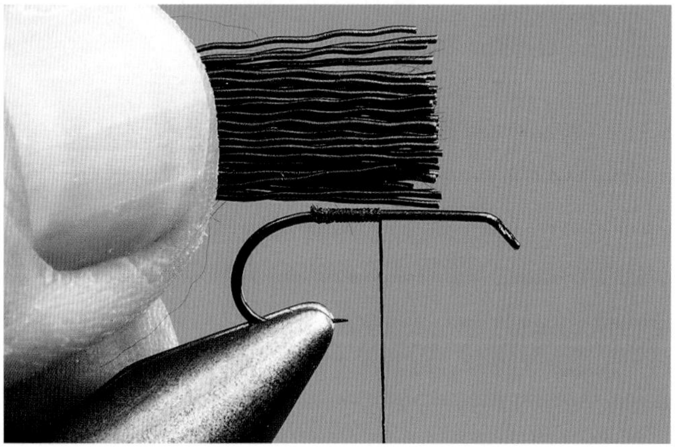

**2.** Select a tuft of coarse dyed black deer body hair. Hair selection is important to ensure good floating capabilities. You don't want hair with fine, thin fibers. Position hair above hook shank midpoint, then bind on top of the hook with butts facing forward.

**3.** Make three evenly spaced turns of tying thread toward the hook bend. Make sure the hair is firmly attached to the hook shank.

**4.** Wind thread forward, maintaining the three "floatation billets." The thread now rests at the hook midpoint. Snip off the excess butt hairs, being careful not to cut your tying thread.

**5.** Grasp deer hair and pull it forward to create the ant's large abdomen. Make a wrap of thread over the hair and secure firmly to hook shank.

**6.** Pull back the deer hair and position the tying thread a short distance up the hook shank.

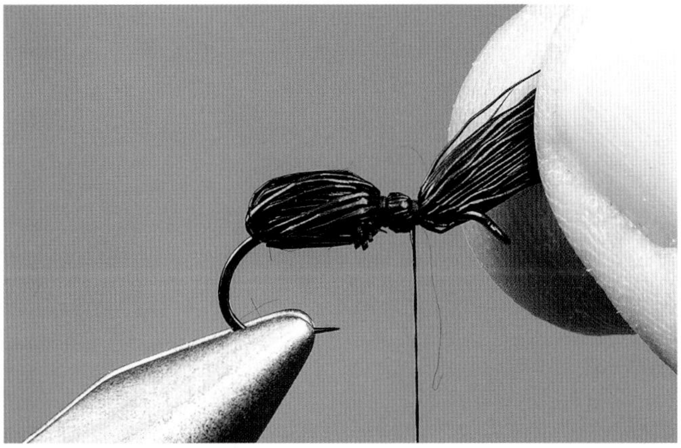

**7.** Pull the deer hair firmly forward, then with your other hand throw a couple wraps of thread over the hair, creating the small middle bulge. You want to make sure that you've created a distinct bulge. These little "floatation billets" will aid in helping to float the fly. You can accentuate the bulge by straddling the hook shank, in front, with your thumbnail and middle finger nail. Once your nails are placed on the hook shank in front of the bulge, you can gently force the segment back.

**8.** Again, pull back the deer hair and advance the thread a short distance up the hook shank.

**9.** Pull deer hair firmly forward, then throw a couple wraps of thread over the hair, creating the third small bulge segment.

**10.** Lively tied his original Carpenter Ant with legs coming off the head area of the fly, flaring back. (In later years, he positioned the legs at the middle of the body). Pull back four or five deer hair fibers on each side of the hook to create the ant legs. The legs should extend back to the abdominal bulge. Snip off any excess deer hair that is projecting forward.

**11.** Wrap thread over the trimmed hair butts, then snip off the leg hairs on each side of the ant.

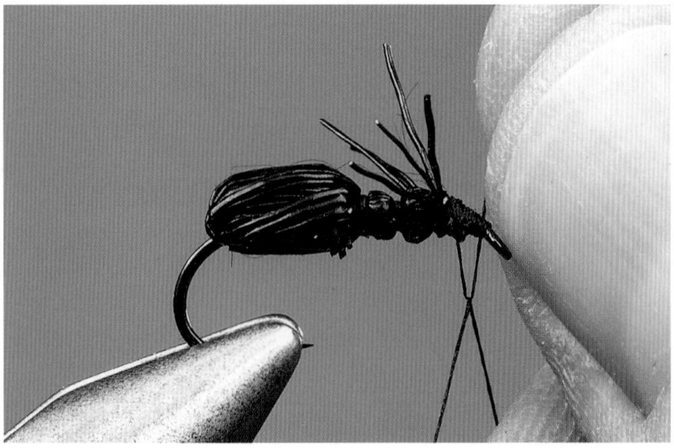

**12.** Throw a whip-finish knot to secure the head.

**13.** Add a drop of head cement.

**14.** The completed Lively Carpenter Ant, my sole go-to terrestrial pattern during summer trout fishing.

# CHAPTER 5

# Casual Dress

## *Nymph*

*"It was a tremendous success, as witness [sic] the fact that while we landed only four browns of 2 to 4 pounds, we shared in hooking six fish, all of which we were certain exceeded 10 pounds."*

—*Polly Rosborough,* Tying and Fishing the Fuzzy Nymphs, *1965*

E. H. "Polly" Rosborough's name instantly came to mind when considering the West Coast greats—and their patterns—that I wanted to include in *The Founding Flies*. I never met Polly, but I was aware of his work as far back as the late 1960s, during my first couple of years at the fly-tying vise.

Nearly all the mail-order fly-fishing catalogs—the few that existed in those years—mentioned Polly's book on their short list of must-have titles. I purchased my copy of *Tying and Fishing the Fuzzy Nymphs* from either Eric Leiser's Fireside Angler supply house in Melville, New York or Buz's fly shop in Visalia, California. Those were my go-to supply houses in my teenage years. At any rate, the book first occupied a place on my tying bench many years ago.

My good friend Ed Ostapczuk, also a product of the 1960s fly-fishing era, is still a big fan of Rosborough's book and his patterns. Ed isn't so rigid that he won't try contemporary patterns. However, he hasn't given up on the classic patterns that have produced well for decades. Like many of us, Ed was struck by Polly Rosborough's book and the series of "fuzzy nymphs." In correspondence, Ed shared his story:

Polly Rosborough's Casual Dress is a buggy-looking pattern that was first fished on Oregon's Deschutes River. He called it an "accidental fly," thrown together with muskrat fur in a most "casual manner."

Ed Ostapczuk, fishing the Esopus Creek in the Catskill Mountains of New York. Ed has been fishing the Casual Dress for decades on his beloved nymph waters with great success. He has netted brown trout, brook trout, and rainbow trout on the fly.

In 1971 I acquired an Orvis edition of Polly Rosborough's *Tying and Fishing the Fuzzy Nymphs*. The very title of this little book, "fuzzy nymphs," sounded intriguing. I was truly impressed with the generic, well-thought-out patterns that Rosborough wrote about. And Polly's Casual Dress quickly earned a revered place in my box of nymphs, maintaining such to this day. I like the fact that the pattern is fishy-looking and generic in nature, tied with muskrat. It can pass for a mayfly, stonefly, or caddis. The collar pulsates and breathes life as this fly moves through the water column, exciting lethargic trout.

Polly's book wasn't the first that delved into nymph fishing, something that I discussed in *The Founding Flies*, but many of his patterns were unique in their simplicity. Polly's book was different, and I've always believed that he was instrumental in really getting fly tiers interested in tying these types of fly patterns. His instructions were not presented in colorful, macro photography with detailed, easy-to-follow, step-by-step tutorials. It was sometimes difficult for me, as a kid, to follow his tying techniques. But his work was interesting and enlightening—and still is. His Casual Dress is one of the easiest patterns to master and one of his most effective.

The pattern was born on the Deschutes River in October of 1960. Polly called it an "experimental accident," a creation haphazardly thrown together in a most "Casual" manner. Armed with three of the extra-fuzzy-looking nymphs, Polly stepped into the Deschutes where it enters Wickiup Reservoir and hammered some pretty impressive fish measured in pounds, not inches. Polly's simple muskrat-fur nymph soon became one of his standards.

It's intriguing how such a simple pattern—a hook with wads of scraggly, unkempt muskrat fur and some fuzzy black ostrich herl at its head—could be so effective. The reason, I believe, is that it appears to have the quality of "insectness."

The quality of "insectness" was a concept that well-known outdoorsman and fly angler Ted Trueblood coined from his own observations concerning the effectiveness of other simple fur-body fly patterns. It's interesting yet not surprising that Trueblood wrote the foreword to Polly's book. He recognized the importance of nymphs and often wrote about his own experiences with ragged, fur-bodied patterns such as his Otter

Shrimp. Details concerning the "insectness" theory are discussed in the Trueblood chapter in *The Founding Flies*. In brief, what he said was that a fly pattern can be effective if it *appears* to be insect prey. In other words, if something looks buggy, there's good probability that a fish will pounce on it. The Casual Dress no doubt *appears* to be prey—an insect or other invertebrate.

## Fishing the Casual Dress

My spring- and fall-season fly boxes are filled with Casual Dress nymphs. While Rosborough liked the fly tied on a size 4 hook, it works in smaller sizes, down to size 14. Fishing an easy-to-cast, small-size Casual Dress in a boulder pool, letting it sink then float dead-drift, brings me great joy. Especially when, as a result of my effort, there's a tug on the delivery end. A fat trout with a Casual Dress or other classic nymph pattern dangling from its mouth always brings a smile.

Ed Ostapczuk, one of the most accomplished fly anglers I know—I like to call him "Dean of the Esopus Creek," in the Catskill region of New York—also enjoys fishing the Casual Dress during the spring season. Ed shared with me his tactic for fishing the pattern, a standard in his box that he won't likely ever abandon:

> Typically I fish a large, heavily weighted pattern slow and deep in the cold water of early spring. Mostly I'm only fishing my leader on a very short line, dead-drifting a couple feet upstream of me with my rod held high to minimize drag. The slightest hesitation and I strike, many times rewarded with a trout, always grateful for Polly and his fuzzy nymphs.

## Tying the Casual Dress

Rosborough tied his Casual Dress on big 3XL, 2X stout, sproat-bend hooks, such as the Mustad 38941. I have a good supply of the 38941, since it's always been a favorite of mine for large nymphs. However, use your preferred nymph hook model.

Muskrat fur is readily available. If you're planning on tying lots of the Casual Dress or similar muskrat nymph patterns, do yourself a favor and purchase a complete skin. You will be surprised how inexpensive a complete skin is, compared with the price of small muskrat skin patches. You can get complete skins from hide and fur establishments. I purchase all my natural fur from Moscow Hide and Fur, located in Moscow, Idaho.

An additional advantage of purchasing complete skins is that you will get the backs of the animal skin that have the guard hair optimum for tying the Casual Dress. If you purchase random small pieces of muskrat, you might not receive the fur that's best for tying the pattern. If you prefer to order a few small muskrat pieces, make sure that you let your fly tying material supplier know that you want sections with plenty of guard hairs, preferably from the muskrat's back section as opposed to the belly section.

Rosborough's technique was to cut off an adequate amount of muskrat fur, then jumble it into a rough mix, with guard hairs pointing in every direction. He didn't just spin it on tying thread, readying it for the fly body in the usual way. He placed the fur into a loop of thread that was coated with cement.

The "spinning loop" was twisted and wound on the hook shank. Using the loop helps keep the fur from falling off the thread when the fly body is being wrapped. Without this technique it's hard to dub the fur mix and end up with the desired scraggly-looking fly with guard hairs sticking out all over the place.

In the steps that follow, I created two separate spinning loops—one for the abdomen and one for the thorax collar area. I don't always use the spinning loop technique, especially on smaller hook sizes. As long as your end product appears disheveled and untidy, you can depart from using the spinning loop technique.

### DRESSING

| | |
|---|---|
| **Hook:** | #4-10 Mustad 38941 |
| **Thread:** | Black 6/0 UNI-Thread |
| **Tail:** | Muskrat with guard hairs |
| **Body:** | Muskrat with guard hairs |
| **Collar:** | Muskrat with more guard hairs than abdomen area |
| **Head:** | Black ostrich |

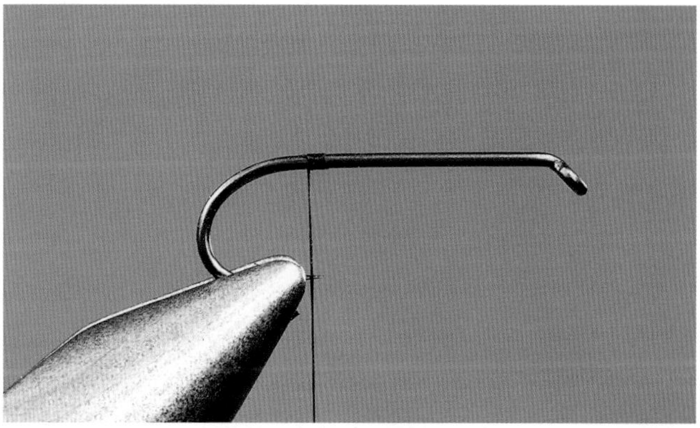

**1.** Bind thread on the hook shank approximately above the hook point. You can weight the nymph, if preferred, with a few wraps of lead wire along the hook shank. (See the A.P. Black Beaver chapter for a good technique.)

**2.** Cut a thick section of muskrat back fur that includes the guard hairs.

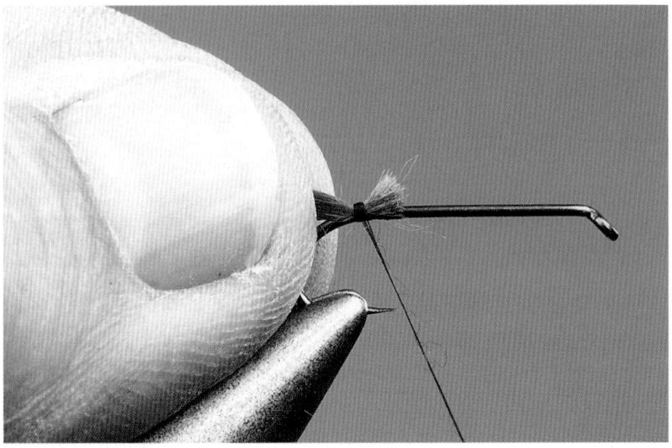

**3.** To create the tail, tie in the muskrat by laying the underfur on top of the hook shank with guard hairs facing to the rear.

**4.** Take a 5-inch section of 6/0 black tying thread and double it, forming a loop. Tie the two thread ends in at the tail position. It's not shown here, but it's best to coat the insides of the loops with some head cement to help keep the fur in place.

**5.** Cut additional sections of muskrat that include plenty of guard hairs. Place the cuttings into a medium-size plastic box—shoebox size—and mix the guard hairs in thoroughly with the underfur. You're going to want a dubbing mix that's rough in appearance. Create a pile of dubbing that's about three inches long and about an inch wide. Place the fur strip inside the thread loop.

**6.** Move the regular tying thread forward about three-quarters of the shank length in a position ready to accept the body dubbing. With hackle pliers, grasp the end of the loop of thread that now contains a layer of muskrat with guard hairs pointing in all directions, pull tight, then twist the fur and thread into a rope.

**7.** Wrap the rope forward on the hook shank, twisting the rope as you progress to the end point. Maintain gentle tension on the rope as you're twisting and moving up the hook shank. Secure the rope with tying thread and the excess snipped away.

**8.** Tie in a second loop of thread. Add some head cement to the inside of the thread loop. In this loop, add muskrat that contains many more guard hairs.

**9.** Twist the second loop into a rope, with lots of guard hairs, and wrap forward—toward the hook eye—a distance four-fifths of the hook shank length.

**10.** Clip the second fur dubbing rope excess then tie in a black ostrich herl at the forward end of the fur body. Use three or four herls for large-size hooks.

**11.** Wrap the herl to a point just short of the hook eye.

**12.** Snip off the excess herl, being careful not to snip the tying thread.

**13.** Secure the head area with thread wraps then throw a whip-finish knot. You can gently stroke the small herl flues to the rear when tying off the fly.

**14.** Add a drop of head cement to the fly.

**15.** The Casual Dress, an effective pattern since its creation in 1960, is now complete.

CHAPTER 6

# Conover

## *Dry fly*

*"The fish turned and headed down through Hendrickson's. By that time I had quite an audience cheering me on. The scenario lasted a good twenty minutes, and I finally beached the trout, admiring its 17 inches."*

—*Mike Valla,* Tying Catskill-Style Dry Flies, *2009*

The tail of Barnhart's Pool on New York's Beaverkill River has always been a favorite stretch of dry-fly water. Barnhart's is a long pool that eventually dumps into Hendrickson's, a picturesque, popular pool that attracts fly anglers because of its proximity to the road.

In *Tying Catskill-Style Dry Flies*, I described a beautiful June 1972 Catskill day on Barnhart's when, as a newly minted high school graduate, I was casting a small Conover over a trout rising in shallow water against the far bank. The nice 17-inch brown, my largest catch to date, brought congrats from the crowd down in Hendrickson's, where I finally beached it. It sipped in my Conover worked off a 7-foot Leonard that a guy who had too many Scotch-and-waters the night before handed to me as a graduation present.

The Conover is still a great pattern and a few of them always occupy my fly box. The pattern goes back to at least the 1930s when Scotty Conover, a member of the Brooklyn Fly Fishers Club on the Beaverkill River, designed the pattern. Conover had difficulty seeing darker-shade flies when fishing at dusk. His new creation, tied with lighter-shade badger hackle, proved perfect for fishing during the late evening hours. Conover requested that Catskill fly tiers Walt and Winnie

**The Conover was born in the Catskill Mountains of New York State. Catskill fly tiers Walt and Winnie Dette tied the pattern for Scotty Conover, a member of the Brooklyn Fly Fishers Club. The fly was born in 1934.**

Barnhart's Pool, on the Beaverkill River in the Catskill Mountains region of New York State, has always been favorite dry-fly water. A long pool, it eventually spills into Hendrickson's, the next pool downstream. It gave up a 17-inch brown trout to a Conover that was rising near the bank, shown at the far right of the photo near the overhanging hemlocks. VALERIE VALLA

Dette exclusively tie the pattern for him. Conover eventually allowed the Dettes to fill their fly bins and offer it for sale to all fly-anglers.

Winnie was a big fan of the Conover, a fly that was long ago the go-to pattern for fishing local caddisfly hatches but also a general all-purpose "searching" pattern. Among the myriad caddis patterns featured in Larry Solomon and Eric Leiser's now classic *The Caddis and the Angler* (1977) is the Conover. It's a simple fly that brought many trout to the net during caddis emergences on the Beaverkill long before the popular contemporary patterns were tied on our tippets.

## Fishing the Conover

While the Conover is no longer a popular fly for fishing caddis emergences, it is still a great fish-taker. Its longer hackle makes it a perfect fly to cast over riffles where it can be skittered and hopped, causing enough commotion to get a trout's attention. Fishing the fly as a searching pattern, it imitates no specific insect but instead appears as a fluttering bug. It's great fun to cast the fly across and downstream, letting it swing then skipping it over the water surface with short twitches. There's nothing more exciting than to witness a trout slam it on the twitch. Its golden badger hackle makes it easy to spot on the water at dusk; it's a good fly to fish in the evening regardless of water type—slow pools or riffles.

## Tying the Conover

It's puzzling why such an easy fly to tie has dropped off the radar; most fly anglers have never heard of the pattern unless they happen to be close to Catskill region waters or fly fishers that are familiar with its history. But even then, there's not a heck of a lot of interest in tying this fly these days. I hope to change that feeling.

Some have mentioned that it's sometimes difficult to obtain an ample supply of badger hackle capes. You may have to do some searching and asking but I've experienced no difficulty in getting my hands on badger hackle. That was also the case during the early years when the fly was popular.

In *Tying Catskill-Style Dry Flies* I told the story of my first encounter with badger capes. I was only fifteen years old when Walt and Winnie Dette took me in as a houseguest for a little over a week then, and again on other occasions over the summer.

I was eager to learn all that I could about materials and tying methods. When talk turned to hackle, Walt Dette got up from the backyard picnic table. "You want to eat your heart out?" he chuckled. "Let me show you something." He went into the house and returned with tin boxes full of Chinese badger capes and dumped them on the ground, at my feet. I did eat my heart out; I had never even seen a badger cape. I remember Walt said he paid only twenty-five cents a cape for them, from a supplier in New York City.

Badger capes cost more than a few cents these days, but there's an easy alternative that you can try, in a pinch. Hackle the fly with ginger shade instead of badger. Using a fine tip, black indelible pen, carefully touch the hackle barbs at their bases near the hackle quill. Dab the hackle barbs. Be careful not to overdo it, as the ink will wick up too high. You want the black shade to reach slightly above the quill wraps. This will simulate the appearance of a wrapped badger hackle, with its black center. However, it's best to get your hands on some good badger hackle and tie the fly in its original form.

As is true with many early trout flies, the Conover has undergone little change over the years. While the use of badger hackle on the Conover is no different, the body dubbing used to tie original Conovers was eventually changed. It's unclear why the original body material blend was simplified.

The original blend consisted of rabbit fur, lambs' wool (or seal fur), and dyed scarlet crewel wool. For her own fishing purposes, during caddisfly hatches, Winnie sometimes tied the body with light green dubbing.

## DRESSING

| | |
|---|---|
| **Hook:** | #12-18 Mustad 94840 |
| **Thread:** | Tan 6/0 UNI-Thread |
| **Tail:** | Cream |
| **Body:** | Gray muskrat fur blended with red Shade 230 Patons Classic Wool Yarn |
| **Hackle:** | Golden badger, preferably without black edges on the hackle barbs |

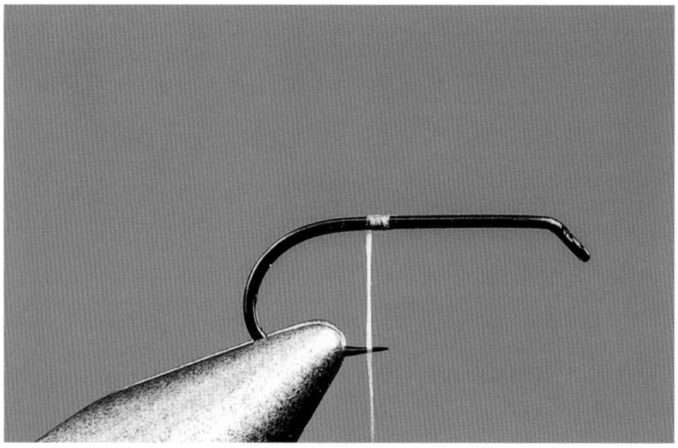

**1.** Attach tying thread to hook shank.

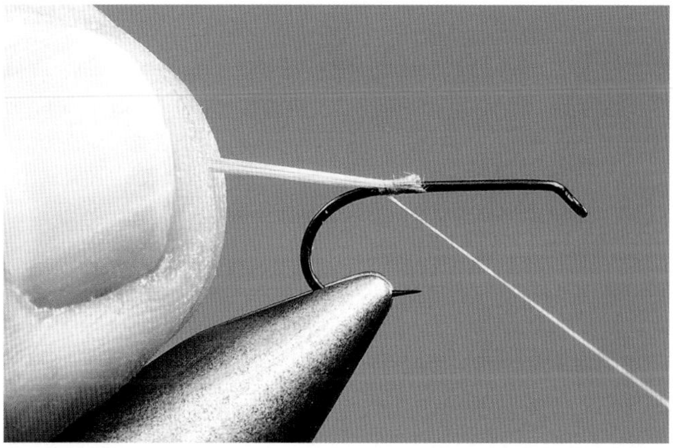

**2.** Select long, stiff, dark cream-shade hackle barbs for tailing. Tie the barbs on the hook shank at a point directly above the hook barb.

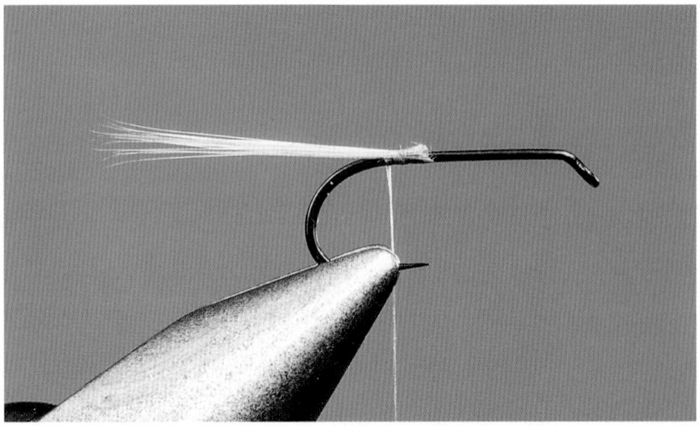

**3.** Conovers are tied with long tails, somewhat longer than the hook shank. Select the stiffest hackle barbs possible for Conover tailing.

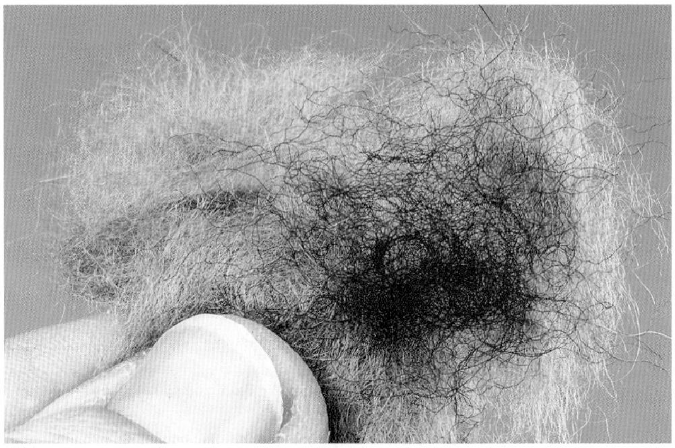

**4.** Prepare the body dubbing by first blending a small quantity of red wool yarn or lambs' wool. Cut a length of wool yarn into small pieces, maybe an inch in length. Place the small pieces into a blender and then mix for a couple of minutes. You'll end up with red dubbing. Blend a larger quantity of muskrat fur, leaving out any guard hairs. You'll end up with muskrat dubbing. Your next step will be to combine the two materials into a uniform dubbing blend.

**5.** Blend small quantities of red wool with muskrat until you arrive at the proper shade. Winnie Dette referred to the shade as "heathery gray claret."

**6.** Tease the blended dubbing into a spindle, then attach to hook shank at the tail. You can add dubbing to the thread using your own method or the "spindle" technique, shown here, used by the Dettes and other classic Catskill-school fly tiers. It's sometimes easier to achieve a smooth, tapered body using the spindle technique; that's what I like most about it and why I've always used it. There's nothing wrong, of course, with adding small quantities of dubbing to the thread in increments.

**7.** If you're using the spindle method, roll the dubbing spindle onto the tying thread, and then wind forward in the direction of the hook eye.

**8.** Carry the dubbing forward, leaving an adequate distance behind the hook eye to accept the hackle winds. Strive for a nice, tapered dubbing body.

**9.** Select one or two badger hackles, depending on hook size, and secure to hook at forward end of the body. Hackle should have longer barbs than you would normally select for the given hook size. I shoot for two and a half times the hook gap distance. Winnie Dette always made a point that the hackles should have the dark centers along the quill stem but she also liked hackles that don't have the black markings at the edges of the hackle barbs. However, a late 1930s example of her Conover showed the black hackle barb ends present. You can sometimes find great Conover badger hackles on rooster saddles. An alternative, should you have difficulty locating good badger hackle, is to simply wrap the hackle with a light ginger shade then carefully darken the center down near the hook shank with a black indelible ink pen.

**10.** Wind your oversize hackle to a point short of the hook eye.

**11.** Throw a whip-finish knot at the head.

**12.** Add a drop of head cement.

**13.** The completed Conover, with its oversize hackle and long tails.

Willowemoc Creek, a tributary of the Beaverkill River in the Catskill Mountains of New York, served as a testing stream for many founding flies, such as the Conover. Dark Coty dry flies perform well on the stream.

# CHAPTER 7

# Dark Coty

## *Dry fly*

*"The flies are really off-springs of the Blue Dun and Iron Blue Dun. Quite a number of years ago Victor Coty, who makes a specialty of taking outdoor movies, was confronted with the problem of finding a fly that would work on the still waters of the Ausable"*

*—Ray Bergman,* Trout, *1938*

Victor Coty was experimenting with new fly patterns that would prove effective on Ausable River, a popular trout stream that tumbles through the Adirondack Mountains in New York State. His goal was to tie a fly that matched the darker dun-shade mayflies that typically emerge on East Coast waters in April and May.

Two common naturals are the Quill Gordon (*Epeorus pleuralis*) and the Hendrickson (*Ephemerella subvaria*). The Hendrickson emergence on the Ausable River brings many fly anglers to its beautiful stretches in the Wilmington, New York area. It isn't surprising that Coty was looking for new dark gray patterns that would perform well for the early-season Ausable hatches.

Coty first experimented fishing a Blue-Gray Bivisible, an all hackle pattern. The "bivisibles"—and there are several shades—are visible to both the trout and the angler. The Gray Bivisible is mostly dark dun hackle tipped in the front with white hackle wraps—making it easy to spot on the water. The fly produced well for Coty but the results still didn't satisfy his needs.

Coty continued experimenting with dry flies crafted with blue-gray bodies and hackles. What he arrived at was the Dark Coty and Light Coty dry flies. Both use gray shades in their bodies, hackles, and wings. The only differences between the two versions are the hackle shades and the

Vic Coty was in search of a better dry fly to match the early dark mayflies found on the Ausable River, in the Adirondack Mountains of New York State. He collaborated with Ray Bergman in designing the fly, replacing the old Iron Blue Dun and Blue Dun dry flies that were commonly used for fishing during early-season mayfly hatches.

West Branch of the Ausable River, in the Adirondack Mountains of New York. Ray Bergman collaborated with Victor Coty to create a dark-shade dry fly for fishing slower-moving stretches of the river in early season. The Dark Coty served them well when dark gray mayflies were hatching, such as Hendricksons.

hackle point wing shades—light and dark. The bodies are identical, a mixture of blue-gray fur and scarlet wool.

Bergman gave his nod to Coty's pattern although he mentioned in his book *Trout* that it's a fly that is difficult to follow as it floats along on water. But he thought enough of both versions—dark and light—to include them in his book. Both patterns also appear in the book's fly pattern color-plate illustrations.

Neither Bergman nor Coty tied the example of the Dark Coty that I photographed and included in *The Founding Flies*. I couldn't get my hands on an original fly tied by either of them, but I was able to get a fly tied by Catskill-region fly tier Walt Dette. The fly that appears in the book came from a large framed set of Dette dry flies that his daughter Mary insisted I take home so that I could photograph late-1930s examples of Dette-tied dry flies

I drove back home—about three hours away—photographed a number of the flies, then the next day drove back to Roscoe, New York to return the framed set to her. An early example of the Dark Coty dry fly would not have appeared in the book without Mary's gracious offer.

## Fishing the Dark Coty

The Dark Coty is a versatile dry fly that can be fished in a variety of waters—East Coast to West Coast. Its dark gray shade makes the fly useful in most any situation where dark-shade naturals are emerging, particularly during early-season months.

On the East Coast, April and May are prime Dark Coty fishing months. Just as Bergman wrote, it's a great Hendrickson hatch fly. The fly brought results for Vic Coty fishing rivers like New York's Ausable and there's no reason to believe that the pattern wouldn't be just as effective today. You could try fishing the pattern in smaller sizes—16 or 18—when the little *Paraleptophlebia* mayflies, the Blue Quills and Mahogany Duns, are emerging in early season, on both East Coast and West Coast streams.

## Tying the Dark Coty

The original pattern called for a mix of gray dubbing and scarlet wool. I've used a wool-muskrat mix in the following steps, but you might want to experiment and tie the pattern using a synthetic red yarn instead of pure wool. Muskrat fur is a good dubbing, and I still love and use it over any type of synthetic material. However, wool loves to soak up water.

Art Flick, the Catskill-region fly tier who knew Bergman and corresponded with him concerning other dry-fly matters, would never have used wool for dry flies. In his *Streamside Guide to Naturals and Their Imitations* (1947), concerning the use of wool in fly patterns, he wrote that he once asked another fly tier if he ever saw a sheep swim. Using a bit of wool blended with fur from an aquatic mammal, such as muskrat, won't sink a dry fly like it was lead. You'll be coating the fly, as usual, with a good dry-fly floatant. However, there's nothing wrong with using a synthetic substitute in tying your Dark Coty flies. You might also prefer to change the original wing material.

All the early trout fly patterns that were tied with hackle point tips for wings used rooster feathers as opposed to hen. The advent of genetic hackle in the late 1970s was a blessing, but what was lost were the nice rounded-tip hackle points, perfect for wings. Genetic hackle was long and the tips were often too narrow to simulate mayfly wings.

Out of necessity, tiers eventually switched to using the broad hen hackle tips for winging, but many of us still prefer the material that was available prior to the genetic era. Commercial tiers, such as the Dettes, tied flies in such great numbers that the switch was inescapable. However, Walt wasn't happy, at first, with the changeover. I never made the change to hen for flies such as the Dark Coty and others such as the Adams, though I'm sure that day will arrive once my supply of good material is exhausted. However, use hen hackle point tips in tying the Dark Coty if that is your preference.

## DRESSING

| | |
|---|---|
| **Hook:** | #12-16 Mustad 94840 |
| **Thread:** | Tan UNI-Thread |
| **Wing:** | Rooster dun hackle points |
| **Tail:** | Dark dun |
| **Wing:** | Rooster dun hackle points |
| **Body:** | Muskrat blended with small amount of Shade 230 Patons Classic Wool Yarn |
| **Hackle:** | Dark dun |

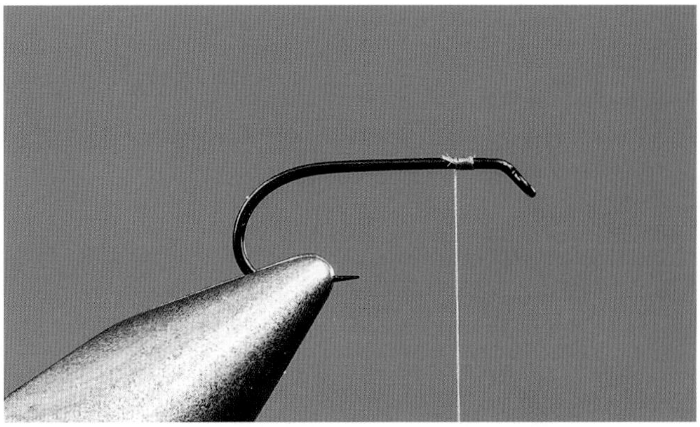

**1.** Begin thread on hook shank set back from the eye $\frac{1}{8}$ inch to $\frac{3}{16}$ inch (depending on the hook size). In this example, as in the Atherton Number One, we're going to finish the fly with a small, clean space behind the hook eye, traditionally used for a turle knot leader attachment. You can also use the two-thirds point on the hook shank as the thread starting point.

**2.** Select two natural dun hackles that have round or broad tips. I've selected rooster hackles here, the traditional feather used for the Dark Coty, but use hen hackle tips if you prefer.

**3.** Position the wing feathers convex side to convex side (shiny side of the hackle to shiny side of the hackle) so that they will flare out when the hackle points are tied in. Run tying thread up between your thumb and index finger and pull down, firmly securing the "pinched" feathers to the hook.

**4.** Snip off the excess hackle butts, leaving the hackle points as wings.

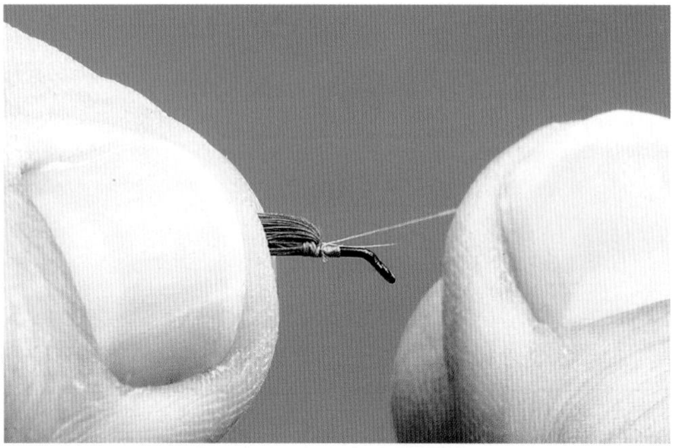

**5.** Make several wraps of tying thread in front of the wing base to secure the wings into an upright position.

**6.** With the wings now in an upright position, add a few more wraps of tying thread to the hackle butts to ready the area for a nice, tapered dubbing body. Encircle the hackle point wing bases to provide additional support and positioning.

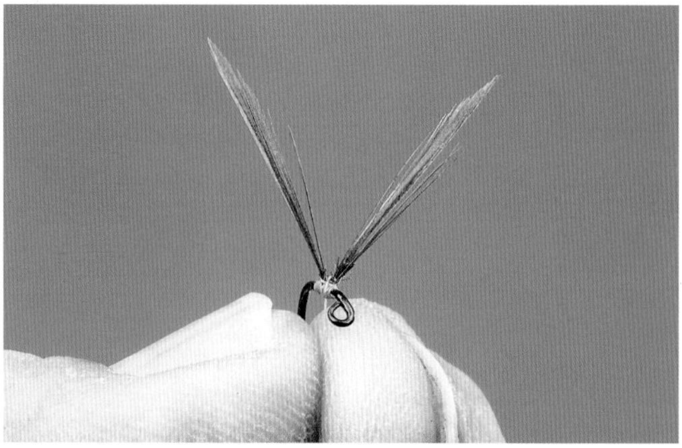

**7.** Divide wings by running tying thread between the upright wings—rear to front then front to rear. The wing attitude will end up as shown.

**8.** For tailing, you'll want to select feathers with stiff, long barbs.

**9.** Tailing hackle fibers are attached at a point on the hook shank above the hook barb.

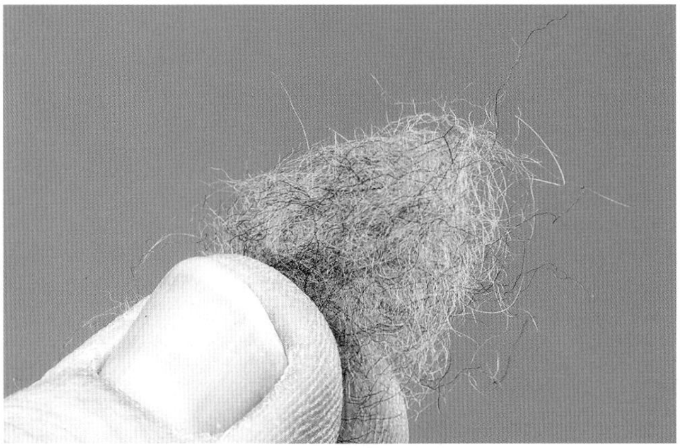

**10.** Prepare body dubbing mix as in the example used for the Conover, in the previous chapter. You can either use the same mix or darken it a bit by adding more muskrat to the blend. In this example, I've used the same Conover blend.

**11.** Add dubbing material to the tying thread in your own preferred method. I've always used the technique taught to me by the Dettes, and also employed by other tiers from the Catskill School. Tease the dubbing into a spindle. Tie in the tapered end at the fly tail. Lift the thread up next to the dubbing. Twist the thread along with the dubbing into a rope.

**12.** Wrap your dubbing rope up to a point just short of the wing bases, ready to accept hackles. The body should be slightly tapered.

**13.** Tie in one or two natural dun hackles, depending on hook size, at the wing base.

**14.** Grasp a hackle and make two to three turns in back of the wing then two turns in front of the wing.

**15.** Secure the hackle just short of the hook eye, being careful not to crowd the eye. Snip off the remaining hackle, making sure not to cut the tying thread in the process.

**16.** If you're using two hackles for a larger-size fly, wind the second hackle through the first up to a point just short of the hook eye. Use a slight weaving, back and forth motion as you wrap the second hackle forward. The weaving will lessen the chance of matting down the first hackle during wrapping. Snip off the remaining hackle end.

**17.** Throw a whip-finish knot to secure the thread head. If you're tying the pattern maintaining a traditional turle knot space behind the hook eye, as in this example, make sure you don't crowd the head.

**18.** Add a drop of head cement.

**19.** The completed Dark Coty, tied in the Catskill style, with the turle knot space—a clean area of hook shank just behind the eye. Most tiers prefer a full head right up to the hook eye; by all means do so if this is your preference.

# CHAPTER 8

# Firehole Number One

## *Dry fly*

*"As a matter of fact I tie a fly for my own use called the Firehole which I use frequently and with success during midge hatches and under certain lighting combinations."*

—*Ray Bergman,* With Fly, Plug, and Bait, *1947*

In his classic book *Trout* (1938) Ray Bergman made the comment that he "never saw more beautiful or accessible dry-fly water" than that on the Firehole River in Yellowstone Park. A trip to the Firehole River proved almost requisite for understanding why Bergman decided to craft his Firehole Number One dry fly, the pattern he described in detail in his follow-up book, *With Fly, Plug, and Bait* (1947).

The water is everything Bergman described, a gorgeous dry-fly stream flowing against a backdrop of bison. Geysers along the river contribute to the scenery; their sulphurous clouds rise in the background causing the angler to occasionally take eyes off the dimples of rising trout.

Yellowstone Park and the Firehole provide many such distractions, particularly at its headwaters, where the Old Faithful geyser erupts every ninety minutes. Bringing my spouse along on a Firehole fishing session caused some interruptions, just as it did for Ray Bergman when his own wife joined him on an outing on that stream. His wife wanted to see Old Faithful; Bergman was more interested in the rising trout he noted as they drove along the river to reach the historic geyser. My wife, Valerie, suggested a better solution to the fishing vs. sightseeing dilemma than perhaps Bergman's wife, Grace, had considered.

**Ray Bergman designed the Firehole Number One dry fly for trout feeding during midge hatches such as those he encountered on the Firehole River in Yellowstone Park. Bergman called it a "somber" pattern that worked well at times big trout were interested in midges.**

The Firehole River at Muleshoe bend, Yellowstone Park. The Firehole served as Bergman's laboratory for developing his Firehole midge patterns. Geysers and bison along the river are sometimes a welcome distraction from dealing with the stream's finicky trout. VALERIE VALLA

The willing and helpful gal that Val is, we were up at five o'clock that morning when we drove into the park from our room in West Yellowstone. It was still dark when we approached Yellowstone Park's entrance gate; the park roads were empty of crowds, and nothing but bison roamed around at that hour. We were on the river at Muleshoe Bend at daybreak on that crisp late-June morning.

The river at Muleshoe Bend is about the loveliest dry-fly water I've ever fished; I can understand why Bergman insisted on developing flies that would work well for him on the Firehole. It's a river that provides challenging dry-fly fishing, its *Baetis* emergences entice both angler and trout. Valerie took care of the photography duties, tiptoeing around the hot springs boiling up through the ground as she made her way along the riverbank with a tripod. I was busy casting loops on the glass-like water.

Just as Ernie Schwiebert warned in his discussion of the Firehole in *Remembrances of Rivers Past* (1972), I reeled in and crawled out of the water talking to myself after a fishless first experience trying to capture a Firehole trout on flies that were too large. Perhaps if I had brought along a supply of Firehole Number One flies in smaller sizes, I would have done better that day.

After I'd had my fishing fix, Valerie smiled when I muttered, "Okay, let's go see Old Faithful now." The vacation crowds were still sleeping as I sat with a cup of coffee on a viewing bench waiting for the show. And, like Bergman, I pretended that I was having a good time. There were trout to be had in the Firehole but sometimes you have to compromise in life, especially if a wife is tugging at your side to do something other than witnessing her husband trying to catch a fish.

## Fishing the Firehole Number One

The Firehole Number One was designed as a tiny dry-fly pattern, perfect for some of the smaller mayflies found on the Firehole River. But its effectiveness in taking fish goes beyond matching miniscule insects on the Firehole; it's a great pattern for fishing *Baetis* and *Paraleptophlebia* mayflies on any water that provides hatches of those two important bugs. However, it's a great pattern tied in larger sizes—up to size 14 and size 12.

The Firehole Number One is perfect for fishing the larger-size, multi-brood, speckled-wing *Callibaetis* hatches on many waters—especially cold, weedy ponds and lakes or slow flowing rivers in the West. *Callibaetis* is much more important on

Western waters, although anglers fishing East Coast, high-elevation, Adirondack-region ponds in New York will sometimes come across the bug.

The Firehole Number One is a great *Callibaetis* artificial; its gray-speckled wings and grizzly hackle offer similarities to the natural insect. I've not heard of or read any reports of fishing this vintage pattern for that insect, but it's my hope that some of my West Coast angling friends—and readers here—will tie it and fish it for *Callibaetis* emergences.

## Tying the Firehole Number One

You should have no problem acquiring the materials required to tie this pattern.

I've noted the Mustad 94842 up-eye hook, since it's always been my favorite for small dry flies. It's the same hook model that I used for the example that appears in the Ray Bergman chapter of *The Founding Flies*. There are many light-wire, dry-fly hooks available; select your favorite.

I've listed muskrat fur for the body dubbing, but you might prefer to use a similar material instead of muskrat. Dark gray red fox underfur is another good choice.

Teal flank feathers are readily available, although many of us who for decades have enjoyed tying with that feather have noticed a decline in obtaining large supplies of the quality that was once available.

### DRESSING

| | |
|---|---|
| **Hook:** | #16-20 Mustad 94842 up-eye |
| **Thread:** | Tan UNI-Thread |
| **Wing:** | Teal flank feathers, finely barred |
| **Tail:** | Black hackle barbs |
| **Body:** | Muskrat fur or dark gray underfur from red fox |
| **Hackle:** | Black and grizzly mixed |

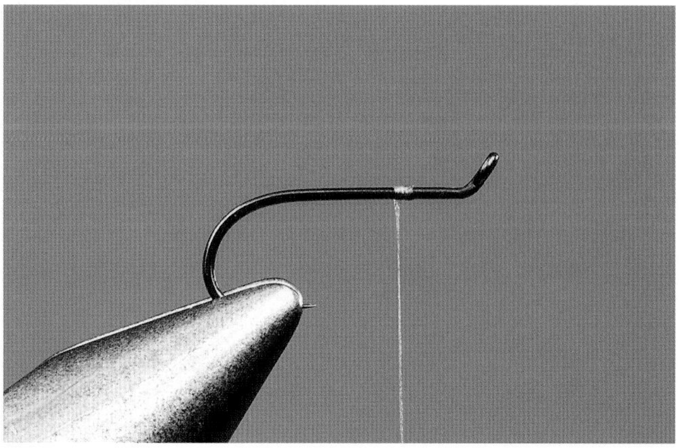

**1.** Attach the thread at the two-thirds or three-fourths point along the hook shank. I've always liked tying midges on small up-eye hooks, such as the Mustad 94842.

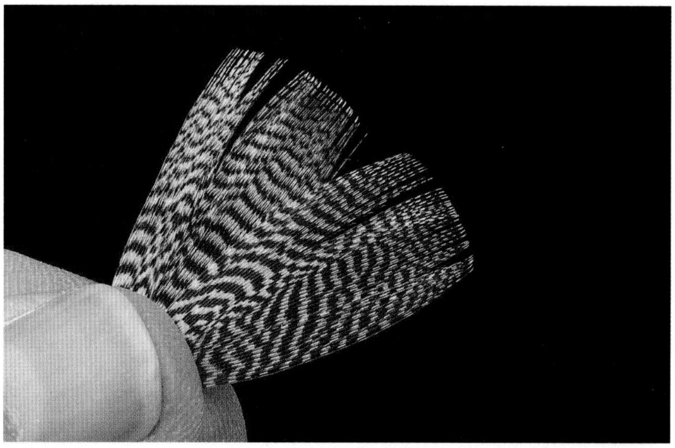

**2.** Select two small teal flank feathers. Since the Firehole Number One is usually tied as a midge fly, I prefer teal flank feathers that have fine markings. Some teal flank is boldly marked, while other feathers from the same bird have finer markings.

**3.** Place the convex sides of the feathers against each other, readying the pair for upright, diverging wings. (If you happen to have my book *Tying Catskill-Style Dry Flies* [2009], you might want to review the chapter on creating upright, divided wings using duck flank feathers. There's a lot more detail in that work concerning crafting flank wings on dry flies.)

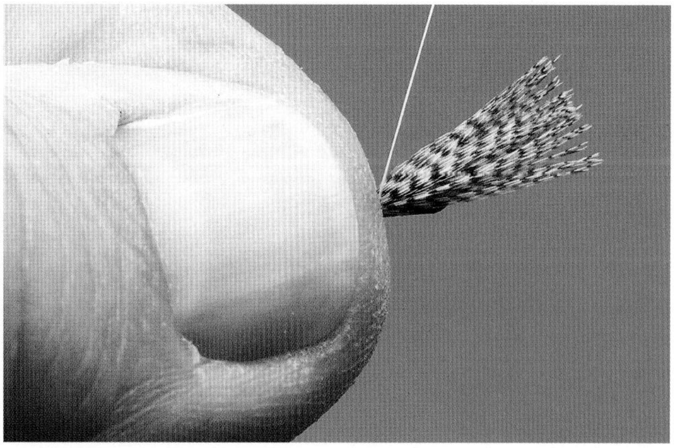

**4.** Position the wing pair on the hook shank with your thumb and index finger. Run the tying thread up between your thumb and finger. Pull thread down, firmly binding the wings to the hook shank.

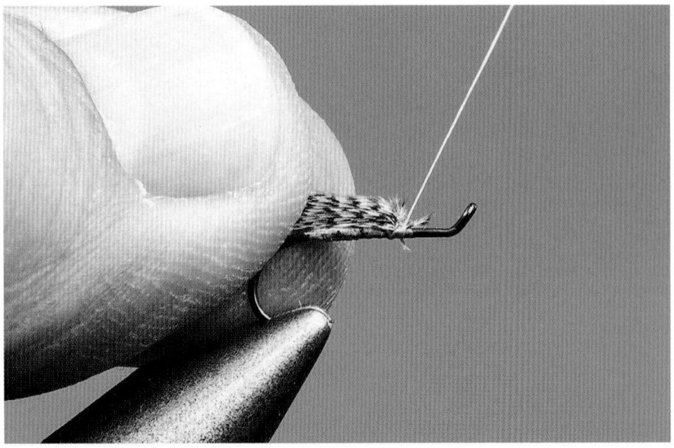

**5.** Wind a few turns of the thread in front of the wings, against the feather butts, to prop the wings into an upright position.

**6.** Encircle the wing pair butts with thread, then divide the wings by running thread from rear to front of wings, then from the front back to the rear. Move the thread back to a point near the hook bend, so it's ready to accept the tailing hackle barbs. (Bergman tied the fly with shorter wings. I'm tying it with towering wings, in the Catskill style.)

**7.** Select a large, dyed black hackle feather that has long, still barbs for tails.

**8.** Bind a few hackle barbs to the hook shank at a point directly above the hook barb. As is the case in most of my dry flies, I prefer long tails, a bit longer than the hook shank length.

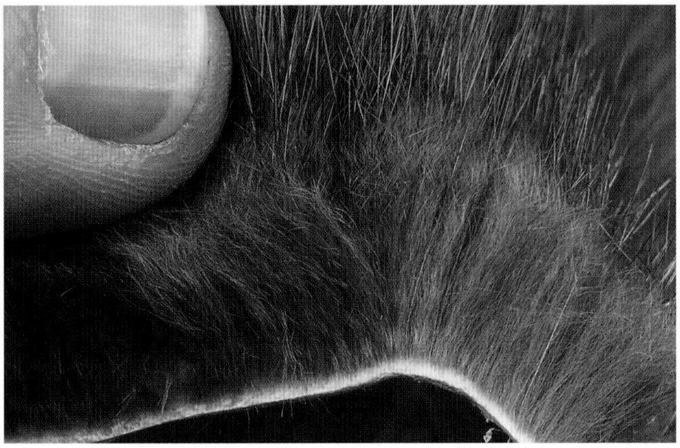

**9.** Cut a swath of dark blue-gray muskrat underfur for the fly body.

**10.** Add dubbing material to the tying thread. In the method shown here, tease dubbing into a spindle. Tie in the tapered end at the fly tail. Lift the thread up next to the dubbing. Twist the thread along with the dubbing into a rope. You can use any method you prefer to add dubbing to the thread. Many tiers prefer to twist and roll dubbing in small increments to the tying thread.

**11.** Wrap the muskrat-fur dubbing to a point just short of the wing butts.

**12.** Select a grizzly hackle and a black hackle and tie in at the base of the wings. Here, I've selected hackles with barbs measuring roughly twice the hook gap. That size is a preference, but is actually characteristic of dry-fly hackle from the Catskill School of tiers. Examples of Bergman's flies followed that early style, given his proximity to the Catskill Mountain streams in New York State. It was the style of his era, and the reality of the non-genetic hackle years, especially when tying small flies like midges. But, again, use the hackle barb length that suits your own preferences.

**13.** Wind the black hackle forward, two or three wraps behind the wing and two or three wraps in front of the wing.

**14.** Use a slight weaving, back-and-forth motion as you wrap the grizzly hackle forward through the black hackle. The weaving will lessen the chance of matting down the black hackle during wrapping. Make sure the hook eye isn't crowded, which is easy to do on small-size hooks.

**15.** Snip off the remaining hackle feathers, secure with a couple winds of thread, then tie a whip-finish knot.

**16.** Add a drop of head cement and the Firehole Number One is completed. The fly was originally tied as a small midge pattern. Larger versions can bring fish to the net, too.

This large Battenkill River brown trout was taken on a Firehole Number One. The fish, named Tethys by the author, eluded capture for several weeks. Tethys is a goddess from Greek mythology, the mother of the great rivers of the world. Tethys was netted at the Grocery Pool on the river near the Vermont border.

CHAPTER 9

# Golden Darter

## *Streamer*

*"When a fisherman sees a great trout tear a quiet pool apart by lunging after a school of frightened minnows, he has reason enough to wish for streamer flies."*

*—Lew Oatman, "Streamer Flies from Nature's Patterns,"* Esquire, *August 1956*

The Lew Oatman chapter in *The Founding Flies* was one of the most enjoyable to tackle. Writing the chapter reconfirmed my own feeling that Oatman didn't receive full recognition for his accomplishments until several years after his death in 1958. It wasn't until Joe Bates published *Streamer Fly Tying and Fishing* in 1966 that the fly-fishing world knew the extent of Oatman's contributions to streamer fly tying. Before Bates's book was published, anglers and tiers were exposed only to brief glimpses of Lew Oatman, the fly angler who fly-fishing author Ernie Schwiebert called "the father of the scientific approach to baitfish patterns."

The 1954 *Family Circle's Guide to Trout Flies*—later reprinted as the *Noll Guide to Trout Flies*—featured seven of Oatman's streamers, including the Golden Darter, but there were no attributions along with the pattern illustrations.

During the 1950s, Oatman wrote three brief pieces for *Esquire* magazine. There's a small photo of the Golden Darter in Oatman's short August 1956 *Esquire* article along with an image of the blacknose dace minnow it imitates. The golden-black stripe along the minnow's body matched Oatman's pattern with its golden badger saddle hackle that highlighted that same anatomical feature.

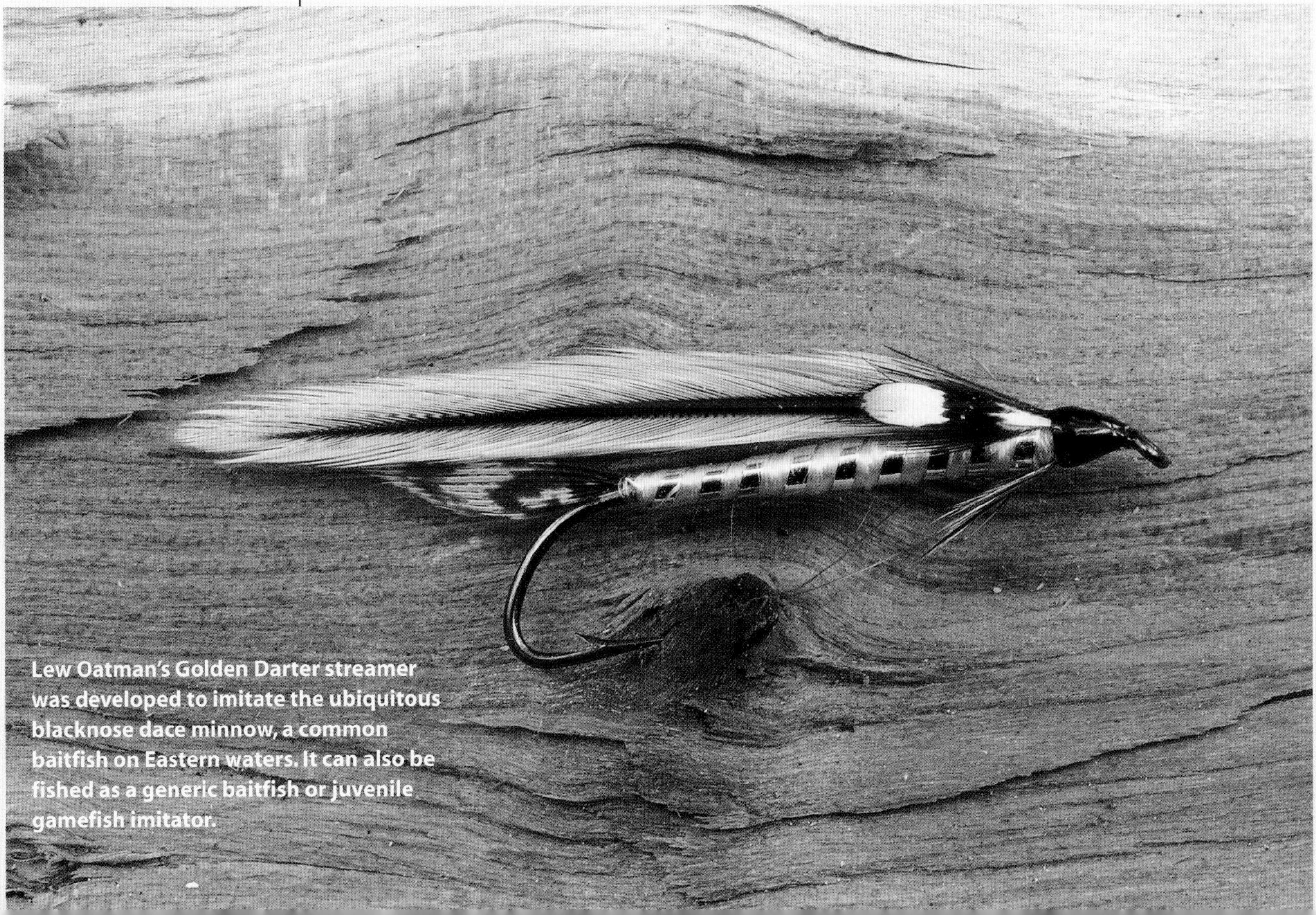

Lew Oatman's Golden Darter streamer was developed to imitate the ubiquitous blacknose dace minnow, a common baitfish on Eastern waters. It can also be fished as a generic baitfish or juvenile gamefish imitator.

The Golden Darter is also a great pattern to fish in early spring and fall on trout-filled ponds such as those found in remote locations in the Adirondack Mountains in New York State. Trolling along the shoreline by slow-rowing a canoe, with a long rod fitted with floating line and a short sink-tip section, can prove effective.

*Field & Stream* magazine fishing editor and book author A. J. McClane provided some exposure to Oatman's baitfish patterns. The dressing for Oatman's Golden Darter, along with short notes concerning the fly, appeared in McClane's short "One for the Book" column in the July 1951 issue of *Field & Stream*. A letter to McClane from Oatman appeared McClane's 1953 *The Practical Fly Fisherman*, describing success with the Golden Darter streamer, and a cousin pattern called the Silver Darter streamer, on a Vermont stretch of the Battenkill River, not far upstream from the New York State border, at Arlington. Oatman landed two good brown trout that day, one 19 inches and another 16 inches.

## Fishing the Golden Darter

The Golden Darter is a good pattern for both trout and bass. It's a good stream pattern but also a good early-season attractor streamer trolled from a canoe, just after ice-out, on small ponds and lakes. In streams, Oatman liked to fish the Golden Darter in slightly discolored water, while he used his Silver Darter pattern in clear water situations.

In his 1951 *Field & Stream* column "One for the Book" that featured the Golden Darter, A. J. McClane offered interesting tactics for enticing trout to a streamer fly. When fishing streams, McClane advised fishing patterns like the Golden Darter in feeding runs situated directly above large, deep pools. McClane's technique allowed the streamer to dart around in the currents and small eddies on its own. Haphazard casting with sudden, quick line strips didn't work nearly as well for him as letting the fly slowly work through the current.

I like to cast streamers quartering upstream, to get the fly down in the water column. When the streamer begins its swing across the current, I strip the line in short jerks. If the water is high and off-color, my tactic is to cast right up against the stream bank, then start stripping as the fly starts swinging downstream. Trout often hug the riverbanks in such conditions.

Trolling streamers by rowing a canoe is a different tactic, most enjoyable on a small pond or lake in early spring or in the fall when trout move into shallower water. While I've never trolled with a Golden Darter, I've used similar streamers tied with badger saddle hackle wings that have brought good results.

My friend and professional colleague John Braico introduced me to canoe trolling with trout flies on a small Adirondack-region trout pond in New York. It was an early ice-out year, in April, and we launched the canoe during a light rain. We were geared up with sink-tip lines as John took care of the rowing duties. John rowed in slow S-curves back and forth along the shoreline, with our lines out 40 feet behind us. It was a raw day but netting numbers of trout made up for the dismal weather conditions.

## Tying the Golden Darter

The Golden Darter doesn't present a lot of problems at the tying vise. The technique is pretty standard. Use two badger saddle hackles for smaller hook sizes and four feathers for large hook sizes.

The wing feathers shouldn't flare out like a feather duster once tied to the hook, a point obvious to those who have tied other featherwing streamers but maybe not so apparent to beginners. If you are using two feathers, the two hackles should be placed against each other with concave sides (dull side of the hackle) against each other.

Let me caution tiers who have not used metal tinsel (my preference) on their flies. The sharp edges can easily cut through tying thread in a hurry, so exercise caution at the point that the tinsel is being secured to the hook with thread wraps.

Use white thread until the point that the body is completed and then switch to black. Otherwise the black thread will show through the yellow floss.

Oatman used golden pheasant tail fibers in early descriptions of the pattern (McClane's 1951 "One for the Book" *Field & Stream* column). However, Oatman's original notes to Joe Bates indicated that a small section of mottled turkey quill slip was used for tailing.

### DRESSING

| | |
|---|---|
| **Hook:** | #6-10 Mustad 3665A |
| **Thread:** | White and black 6/0 UNI-Thread |
| **Tail:** | Small slip of mottled turkey |
| **Rib:** | Lagartun flat gold tinsel (medium) |
| **Body:** | Yellow Danville floss, four-strand |
| **Throat:** | Tip of jungle cock body feather |
| **Wing:** | Two to four slender golden badger saddle hackles |
| **Cheeks:** | Jungle cock eyes |

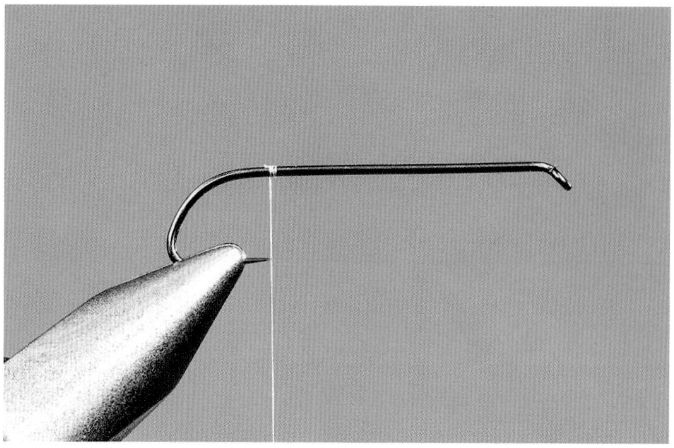

**1.** Attach white thread at the hook bend, directly above the hook point. White thread is used for the first few steps so that black thread, which will be used later for the fly head, doesn't show through the yellow floss.

**2.** Cut a small slip from a mottled turkey quill feather.

**3.** Tie in the turkey quill slip at the hook bend. Then snip off the excess.

**4.** Secure medium flat gold tinsel at the base of the tail with a couple of thread wraps.

**5.** Wind the white tying thread forward, with close wraps, to the hook shank midpoint. For a size 12 Mustad 3665A hook, approximately ten inches of yellow four-strand floss is attached at the midpoint. The length of floss required will be determined by the hook size and model preferred. The floss end is extended forward to a distance that will equal the total body length.

**6.** Continue binding the floss with tight, close thread wraps to its forward end.

**7.** Begin building the tapered body by wrapping the four-strand floss forward, then securing with two thread wraps at a point set back from the hook eye a distance that will allow room for the fly head.

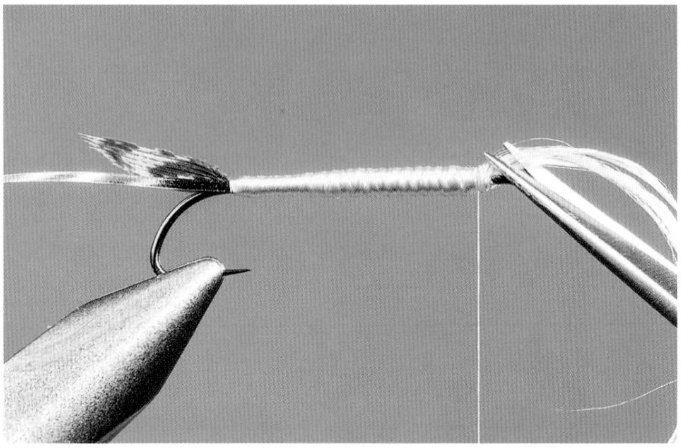

**8.** Wrap the floss back to the hook bend, reverse direction, and wrap back to the fly head position. Secure with a couple turns of thread. Snip off the excess floss.

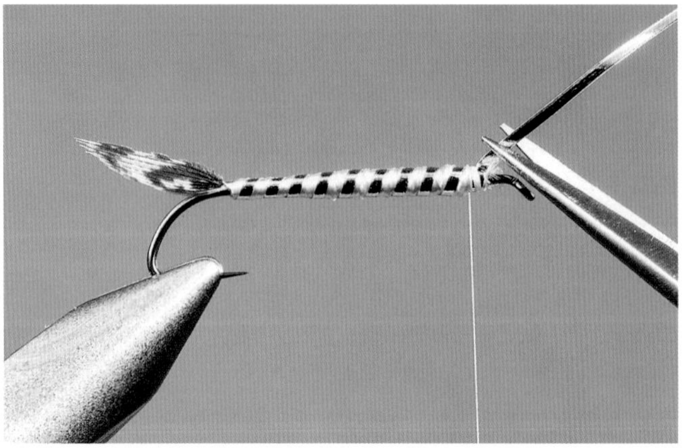

**9.** Bring forward the flat, medium gold tinsel that has been waiting patiently at the hook bend with even wraps around the floss body. Secure it at its front end with a couple of thread wraps. Caution: if you're using metal tinsel (my preference) make sure the sharp edge doesn't cut the tying thread.

**10.** Select a small jungle cock body feather that will be used for a small throat.

**11.** Remove fly from vise, turn upside down, then return fly to vise. Or, if you use a rotating vise, rotate the fly to an upside-down position. Tie off the white thread, snip the end, then start black thread in the same position. Tie in the small jungle cock body feather tip, no longer than the hook gap width. Snip off the excess.

**12.** Select two golden badger saddle hackles or two narrow rooster neck hackles. Make sure that the hackles have a distinct black stripe along the centers.

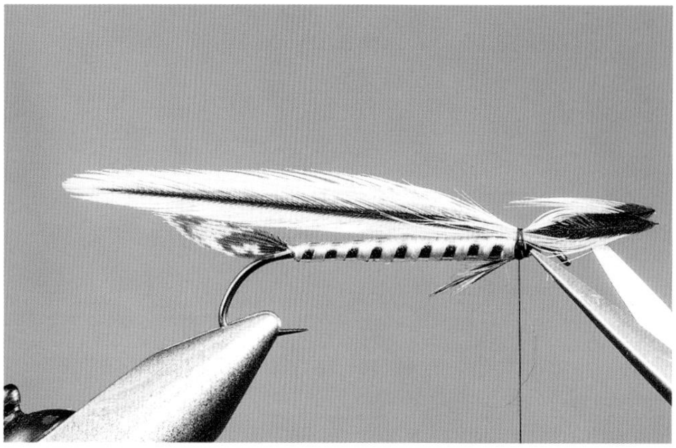

**13.** Place one badger hackle on top of the other, concave side against concave side. The two feathers should not flare out but should be in one plane. Tie the two feathers down on top of the hook shank, dead center. The hackle ends should extend beyond the tail feather. Snip off the excess hackle ends.

**14.** Select two jungle cock eye feathers, one for each side of the fly.

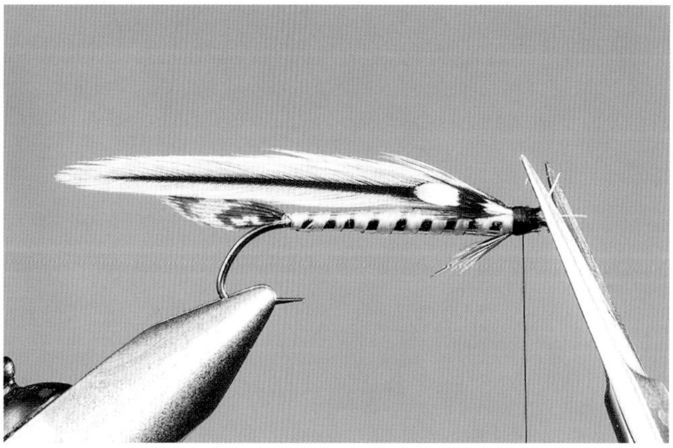

**15.** Tie in the jungle cock eye feathers on each side of the head area, then snip off the excess feather stems.

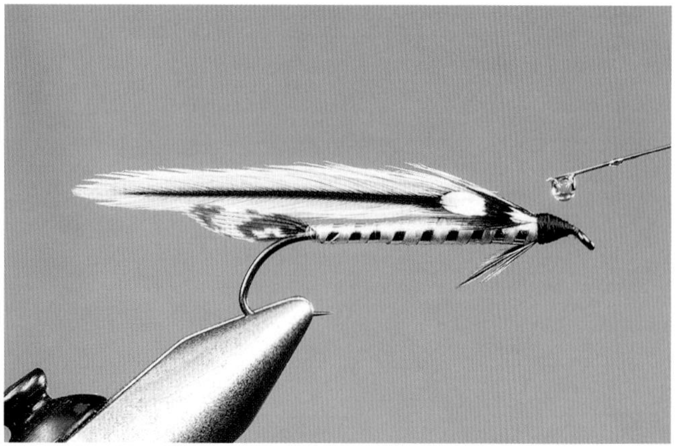

**16.** Build the head with a number of thread turns. Secure the head with a whip-finish knot, then snip off the thread. Add a few coats of head cement to the neatly wrapped fly head.

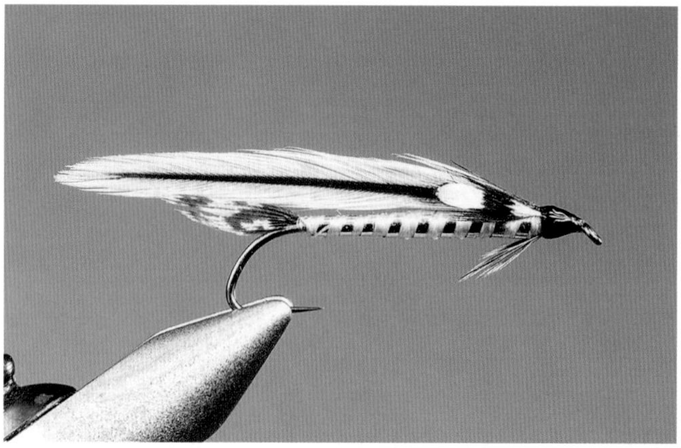

**17.** The completed Golden Darter streamer, a pattern that fishes well in both streams and lakes.

Lew Oatman in the 1950s, tying on a streamer. HERB ERIKSSON

CHAPTER 10

# Jassid

## *Dry fly terrestrial*

*"Carefully observing the lines of drift of feeding fish where the water was silvery, and consequently even the minute particles visible, he saw the jassids disappearing in tiny dimples."*

*—Charles K. Fox, "A New Kind of Fly,"* The Fisherman, *March 1958*

A variety of terrestrial patterns was introduced in *The Founding Flies*—classics that were developed decades ago on Pennsylvania's Letort Spring Run by iconic anglers who, over lifetimes, studied and fished the little stream.

Flies such as Ed Shenk's Letort Cricket and Letort Hopper proved effective for taking the Letort's hypercritical wild brown trout. In his *Modern Dry-Fly Code* (1950), Vince Marinaro, "dean of the Letort," described a peculiar Pontoon Hopper crafted by Charlie Craighead and tweaked by Bill Bennett. Other Letort regulars, such as Marinaro's friend Charlie Fox, also trumpeted newfangled terrestrial trout patterns.

One of the most interesting terrestrial patterns developed by Marinaro and later embraced and reported on by his comrades was unique; the principal material required for its construction was a simple eye feather from a jungle cock fowl, a bird endemic to India.

The small, hard, plate-like eye feathers found on the dorsal neck area of the bird proved perfect for Marinaro's small beetle-like pattern design. It also proved most effective for imitating minute jassid insects, leafhoppers that Letort brown trout routinely sipped off its mirror-like surface. Jassid

**Vince Marinaro developed the Jassid to better imitate beetles and other small terrestrial insects such as leafhoppers. Marinaro theorized that trout peering upward at beetle imitations see only the dimensions of width and length and not the thickness. A single jungle cock eye provided the necessary dimension and resulted in a light, easy-to-cast fly.**

Ed Shenk gazing over the Letort Spring Run in Pennsylvania. Shenk fished many of his creations on the little spring creek. He also fished miniature Jassids on the stream. Shenk first inspired the author to tie the fly.

eaters shunned traditional dry flies, causing much frustration among Letort fly anglers like Marinaro.

The detailed history of the Jassid's development and influences on other anglers who embraced the pattern is described in *The Founding Flies*. Suffice it to say here that Marinaro's on-stream observations that led to the creation of his little Jassids provide an enlightening tale.

Many terrestrial patterns have followed the archetypal Jassid, flies much more sophisticated in their design. However, Marinaro's simple jungle cock-eye terrestrial was, and still is, a great late-summer pattern. It's also a fly that introduced many fly tiers and fly fishers into the world of summer terrestrial trout fishing.

My own introduction to the Jassid didn't come from Marinaro's book. It was Ed Shenk's article in the June 1968 issue of *Field & Stream* magazine, "The Miniature Jassids," that caught my attention. I was six months into fly tying and constantly on the lookout for any fly fishing magazine articles that appeared in the big three—*Outdoor Life*, *Field & Stream*, and *Sports Afield*. None of the myriad fly-fishing specialty magazines of today existed back then.

Shenk's story was a real eye-catcher, and it captured the attention of many fly tiers. It was a story that I have never forgotten, and the opening-page photo of a line of diminutive size 28 flies sitting along the top of a ruler is permanently fixed in my mind. The story had that much impact; fishing size 28 flies was unheard of back then. I remember purchasing a box of the novelty-like size 28 gold Mustad 7995G hooks that Shenk used.

I can't recall when I purchased my first jungle cock cape but it must have been somewhere around 1969 or 1970, just before or shortly after jungle cock cape imports were banned. Prior to the ban, the capes were readily available for around five or six dollars. The only way you could purchase a jungle cock cape after the import ban went into effect, and after existing supplies dwindled, was through the black market. Tiers turned to those awful plastic replica jungle cock eye feathers that were a poor substitute for the real thing. I've always thought that the import ban had something to do with Marinaro's Jassid dropping under the radar. Once jungle cock again became available years later, through legal sources, the simple yet effective Jassid had been long forgotten. Tiers entering the arena in the post-ban years that followed were creating new terrestrial beetle patterns.

Jungle cock is now easily obtained, and you don't need to purchase the AAA capes sought by many salmon fly tiers who need the larger eye feathers for the classic salmon fly patterns. You want the smaller eyes that are obtained from the cape's head and neck area; plenty of good quality, tiny eyes can be selected from less expensive capes.

## Fishing the Jassid

Jassids are designed to float flush in the surface film of quiet water. I've tied and fished Jassids from size 16 down to size 26. I'm sure that Jassids tied down to size 32 would fish well, in certain situations where the water is ultrasmooth and clear. I'm fishing long leaders with 8X tippets on my smaller Jassids, a tippet size that wasn't available in my early Jassid fishing years.

My favorite Jassid rod is a 7-foot, 2-weight, although decades ago I was into fishing Jassids off 6-foot rods on the smaller creeks that I frequented. There was a time that a 5-foot glass rod provided enjoyable Jassid fishing. Jassid fishing is similar to handling tiny Trico patterns. You'll have a ball taking a nice wild brown trout on a classic fly such as Marinaro's Jassid, a pattern still worthy of your box.

## Tying the Jassid

Jassids can be tied with a variety of hackle shades. You can use any shade, but black and ginger were always popular. I don't like to over-hackle my Jassids; the pattern is designed to float flush in the water surface film. You'll notice in the tying steps that I recommend stripping away one side of the hackle quill. By doing that you'll end up with a sparsely hackled fly. You don't need a lot of hackle barbs to float the fly. The jungle cock eye tied flat along the top of the body helps the fly float in the surface film.

While it's the jungle cock nail feather that defines the original Jassid, I've also used Marinaro's basic design in other "Jassid-like" patterns that I was forced into creating during the period of time jungle cock became unavailable. One "Jassid-like" pattern that I still fish is tied with small, barred silver pheasant body feathers dyed green. The feather is placed directly over the hook shank just as the jungle cock nail feathers are positioned on Marinaro's original. It looks good, and fishes great.

Jassids can be tied on a variety of light-wire hook models that are available. I've listed the Mustad 94837, but select the small dry-fly hook model of your choice. It's the model I've used for Jassids for a long time, and I'm using it here mostly out of habit; when my 94837 supplies run out, I'll begin using one of the other good midge hooks that are available. The "Vince Marinaro" hook—a Partridge model developed in 1978—is perfect for tying Jassids. It's an offset, wider gap hook style, a feature Marinaro liked because of its enhanced hooking ability. The straight-eye Tiemco 101 model is another good Jassid hook. Straight-eye hooks are great for patterns tied smaller than size 20.

### DRESSING

**Hook:** #16-32 Mustad 94837
**Thread:** Orange 8/0 UNI-Thread
**Body:** Black, ginger, or brown hackle, palmered
**Wing:** Jungle cock eye

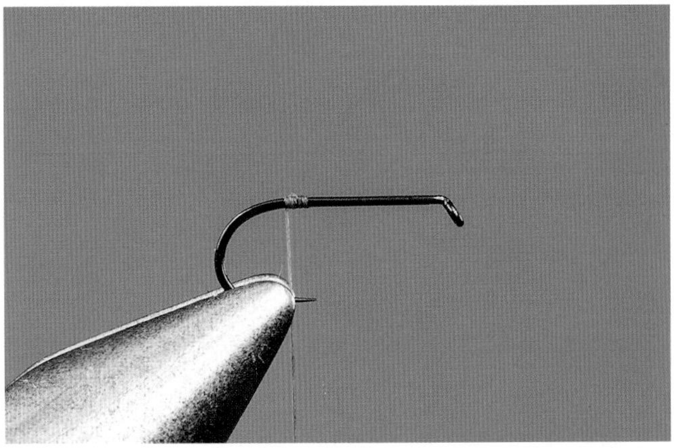

**1.** Attach orange thread at the hook bend. Charlie Fox wrote that Marinaro used orange thread on the original Jassid but you can use most any thread shade.

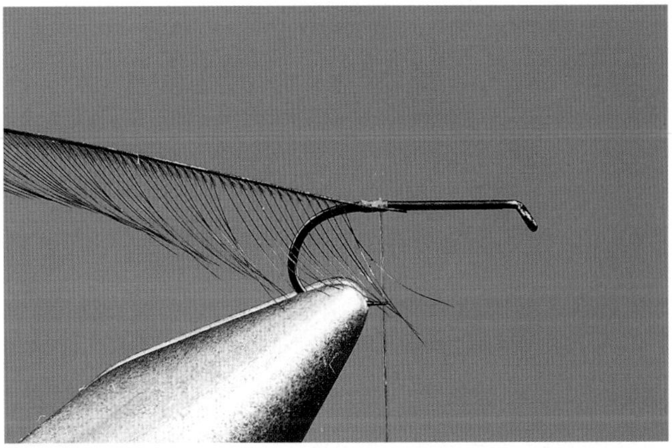

**2.** Select an appropriate small-size black hackle and strip the barbs off the left side of the stem all the way to the feather point, assuming it's being held with the convex side (shiny side) up. Do not tie it in at the tip of the hackle, a weak point, or it will likely break off when you wind it. Ginger hackle is another common shade to use on Jassids and was used on early prototypes.

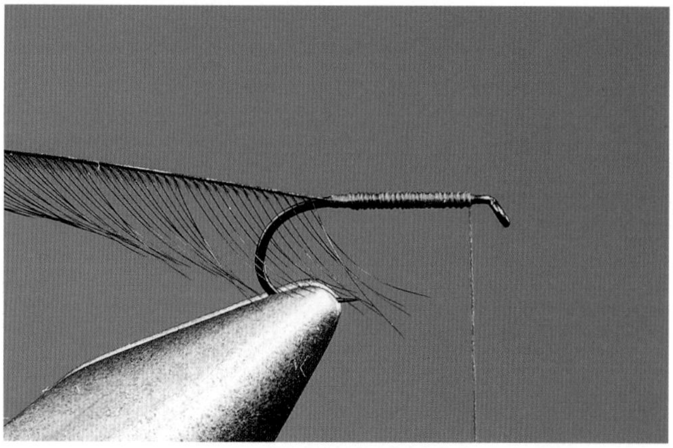

**3.** Wind tying thread to just short of the hook eye. The thread itself will serve as the body. You can add two layers of thread, if you want a little more body substance.

**4.** Grasp the black hackle and wind forward to just short of the hook eye.

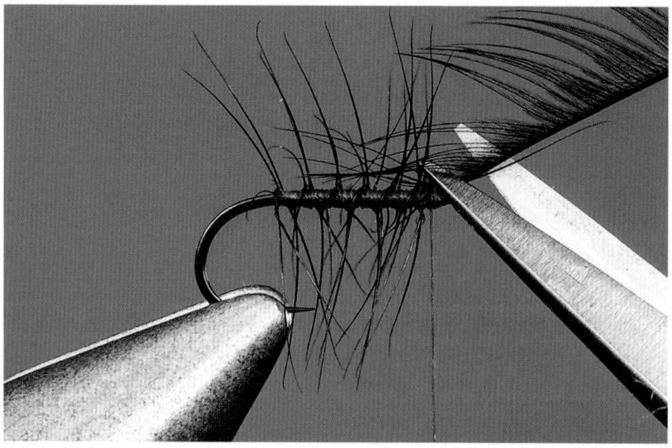

**5.** Snip the remaining excess hackle end. Secure the hackle to the hook with a couple of turns of thread.

**6.** Select a jungle cock eye from the head and neck part of the bird cape. You can use two eyes if you wish, one on top of each other, or by combining two feathers concave side to concave side. But I've always used just a single eye. You don't have to use absolutely perfect feathers to tie your Jassid, but select the ones with the fewest splits, if any at all. Chances are a trout is going to do the splitting for you, with its sharp teeth, so don't get overly concerned about eyes with a few splits. You can coat the eye with an adhesive to strengthen it.

**7.** Tie in the jungle cock eye at the head. You can either trim off the top hackle barbs, so that the eye feather will lie flat, or you can simply stroke the barbs away to the sides of the fly body. I usually just move the barbs that are to the sides so that the eye feather can remain positioned flat over the hackle.

**8.** Making sure you have the eye firmly attached to the hook shank, snip off the remainder, being careful not to snip your thread.

**9.** Cover the end of the jungle cock eye with a few thread wraps, then add a drop of head cement. Marinaro recommended snipping off the underside hackle barbs either into a V or snipping the underside barbs flat. You don't need many hackle barbs sticking out from the sides to float the fly; the jungle cock eye takes care of that duty. Snipping out some of the hackle barbs will enable the fly to float properly in the surface film of the water. However, I've also tied Jassids leaving all the hackle in place.

**10.** The completed Jassid. The fly is an attractive morsel for finicky trout that are feeding on leafhoppers and small beetles. It's still one of my favorite patterns.

Spring creeks are perfect Jassid waters where the pattern can entice superselective trout. Anglers on Spring Creek, located in Caledonia, New York, often fish flies down to size 32.

CHAPTER 11

# Kings River Caddis

## *Dry fly*

*"The evolution of caddis fly patterns is unusual in that it has not followed the geographic romance of the mayfly."*

—*Ted Niemeyer, "The Caddis Explosion"* Fly Fisherman, *April 1977*

Ted Niemeyer's observations in "The Caddis Explosion" explain that mayfly patterns were first developed in Europe, then colonized American waters, then migrated from the East Coast to the West Coast, "changing in style at various stops along the way." However, the caddis patterns took a reverse journey, a path from the West to the East, also changing along the way.

Wayne "Buz" Buszek's Kings River Caddis, a "founding fly," was an archetype of many patterns that evolved over the years. Mottled turkey feathers resemble colorations found in the wings of many caddisfly species. Buz recognized the imitative qualities of mottled turkey and brought his observations to the tying vise, and his caddis was born. The Kings River Caddis is a lovely pattern, an effective fish-getter, and an easy fly to tie.

The Kings River, the California stream that inspired this pattern, was once called *el Rio de los Santos Reyes*—"River of the Holy Kings." In the course of writing *The Founding Flies*, my travels took me around the country to visit some of the waters that made our founding fly patterns famous—their birthplaces. However, the Kings was a river that I was unable to visit until after the book had left the presses and was on the shelves. Two fly anglers from Visalia, California—home of Buszek's fly shop—assisted me with gathering information on Buz and his patterns.

**Wayne "Buz" Buszek, of Visalia, California, created the Kings River Caddis for fishing caddis hatches on Kings River. It was one of the first effective caddis patterns created and soon became popular throughout the country. The Kings River Caddis served as a foundation for many other caddis patterns that were later developed.**

Dave Johnson on the Kings River, California. The scenic river begins its journey in the Sierra Nevada and flows through granitic canyons to a man-made compound behind Pine Flat Dam. The Kings River Caddis was born in the cold-flowing tailrace below the dam where Buz encountered caddisflies that emerged in the summer.

Their help was a great substitute for visiting the Kings River in person.

Don Lieb, now his mid-nineties, knew Buz well, and knows some of the history surrounding his patterns. Don tied flies for Buz's shop after Buz died in 1965; it's his Kings River Caddis that's displayed front and center on the jacket cover of *The Founding Flies*. Then there was Dave Johnson, a Buz Buszek historian who was of immense help to me, through correspondence, over the course of many months during the time I was writing the book. I finally was able to meet Dave several months after *The Founding Flies* was released. And I finally was able to wade the Kings River.

"Welcome to the Kings, home of Buz's Kings River Caddis," Dave Johnson said as he greeted me at the entrance to Avocado Lake on the banks of the Kings River. We shook hands, and then I had a sudden emotional feeling. "I've tied the Kings River Caddis pattern since boyhood days, over forty-five years ago. And I've fished it just as long," I said to Dave. "And now here I am at its home." Buz worked out the pattern to imitate the massive number of caddisflies that once emerged on the Kings River, a phenomenon that inexplicably no longer occurs. He got into some big rainbows fishing the pattern on the river below Pine Flat Dam in the San Joaquin Valley.

It's difficult to recall the exact circumstances of how I first came upon Buszek's pattern but I'm certain I must have noticed it in Buz's fly shop catalog, a simple 5-inch-by-8-inch black-and-white gem that I first had at my side in the late 1960s. There were only a dozen or so fly-tying material mail order houses in all of the country back in those years. Even East Coast tiers would have sent for the catalog.

I ordered the catalog after reading a small advertisement in one of the big three outdoor magazines of that era, probably in *Outdoor Life*. Among all the neat fly-fishing items for sale in the catalog, Buszek's also sold color plates of all of the popular flies sold by the shop. I remember purchasing one of the photos, and it's likely the Kings River Caddis pattern was among those featured on the photograph. The old Orvis catalog may have also shown the pattern in its color plates as it was a popular fly in those years.

## Fishing the Kings River Caddis

My earliest recorded encounter with caddisflies while fly-fishing was May 10, 1970 on the Beaverkill River in the Catskill region of New York State. I'm certain I would have been casting a Kings River Caddis that day. Patterns such as

Kings River rainbow trout. The Kings River no longer offers the massive caddis flight emergences that Buz Buszek encountered. But fly anglers can still enjoy catching rainbows when the water conditions allow for such action.

the Conover, Lenny Wright's Fluttering Caddis, and Larry Solomon's Delta Wing Caddis didn't occupy my fly boxes until a couple of years later. Pennsylvanian Al Troth was already fishing his Elk Hair Caddis, now a popular fly, but none of us back then were even aware of the pattern; it was pretty much still under the radar. (At least I never heard of it or read about it, and the local fly shops bins were empty of that type of pattern at that time.)

By the early 1970s—maybe 1973—I started experimenting with a simple deer hair-wing caddis pattern that I never named. The fly was tied with a fur dubbing body, deer hair flared back from front part of the hook, and brown hackle wrapped just behind the hook eye in the usual dry-fly style. I remember taking a small rainbow trout on the fly, twitched under an overhanging tree. The rest of the memory escapes me. However, the Kings River Caddis was my go-to pattern, for sure.

You could write a book on how to fish caddis dry flies—there are plenty such books out there that discuss the topic. For me, fishing adult caddisflies involves skittering or twitching the pattern across riffles on a downstream drift. One of the nicest and fussiest brown trout I've ever taken on an adult caddisfly pattern was on the New York State section of the Battenkill River, just upstream from Battenville, in around 1978 or 1979.

I was midstream in a long, flat pool just above a long riffle. Caddisflies were buzzing around on that late May evening and fish were rising. My cast was placed directly downstream to a riser, stripping out line to avoid drag as the fly made its way downstream and over the fish's snout. A slight twitch when the fly reached the riser brought the strike. It was a beautifully colored, 15- or 16-inch wild Battenkill brown trout.

## Tying the Kings River Caddis

The fly is an easy tie and should present no real problems at the vise. When tying in the mottled turkey quill slip wing, make sure that you bind the thinner tip-end of the slip. The stronger end of the slip, the area that's clipped right next to the feather quill, should project to the rear. The turkey quill slip is fragile. Buz strengthened the wings with a coat of lacquer. You can also coat the feather with Pliobond-type adhesives to accomplish the same. Buz's original body dubbing was gray-brown raccoon fur. I tie the pattern with a lighter fox fur dubbing, more of a tan shade, as demonstrated here.

Kings River Caddis, tied by Don Lieb. Don tied the fly adhering to the pattern's original form (wings positioned flat over the gray-brown dubbing). Over time, the pattern has been tweaked into a few variations.

## DRESSING

| | |
|---|---|
| **Hook:** | #12-14 Mustad 94840 |
| **Thread:** | Tan or black 6/0 UNI-Thread |
| **Body:** | Tan fox fur or gray brown raccoon |
| **Wing:** | Mottled turkey |
| **Hackle:** | Brown |

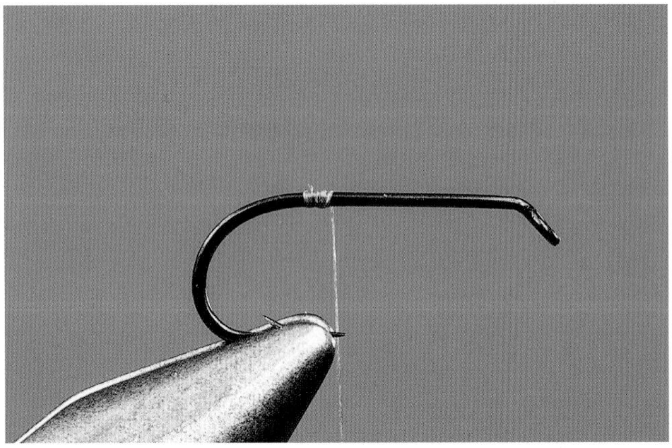

**1.** Thread is attached at the rear of hook shank, directly above the hook point.

**2.** The original dubbing, as tied in the 1950s, was raccoon in a gray-brown shade. You can use that shade (left) or lighten it up a bit using tan-shaded red fox fur dubbing (right), a shade that has been used for many years.

**3.** Attach fur dubbing to thread using your preferred method. The end of the body should begin with a slight taper.

**4.** Wind the body dubbing forward. The completed body should extend up the hook two-thirds the shank length if you desire a heavily hackled fly. You can wind the body a bit closer to the hook eye if you're dressing a more sparsely hackled fly. The body is slightly tapered. The fly is now ready to accept the wing.

**5.** Select and snip a section of mottled turkey quill. I didn't show it here, but to add strength to the otherwise fragile turkey quill slip, it's best to coat it with a flexible cement, such as Pliobond. After coating the slip let it dry.

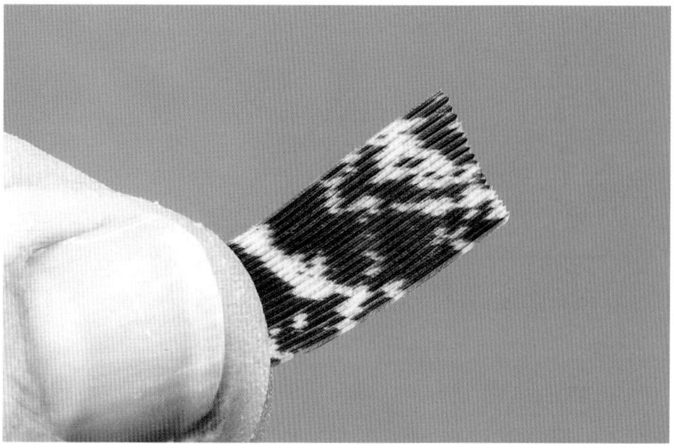

**6.** Since you're going to fold the turkey slip into a tent that will slightly straddle the dubbing body, make sure that the slip is wide enough to create enough of a wing on each side of the fly. A size 12 hook, for instance, would require maybe a 1/4-inch feather slip. It's easy to underestimate the feather width required. Cut your slip so that it's approximately two and a half times the body length, for working room. (This may seem long now, but you're going to snip off some of the rear of the feather in the last step).

**7.** Fold the turkey slip, but not too tight. Straddle the body with the feather and tie it in at the end of the forward end of the body. Important: the heavier part of the feather (the lower part that was clipped closest to the turkey quill) will project *to the rear*; this is the strongest part of the feather. In the photo, my fingers are holding what was the lower part of the turkey feather, right next to the quill.

**8.** The turkey slip, folded and tied in, now straddles the body with an approximate length of two and a half times the body length. Again, this will seem long, but the length will be adjusted later when the end of the feather is snipped off at the rear. Snip off the excess turkey feather that remains in front of the body at this time. In its original form, the Kings River Caddis was tied with the wing flat against the body and not cocked up. To keep the wing attitude flat against the body, tie in the turkey slip on some of the body material and not the bare hook shank. I've always preferred to set my wing up a slight amount—but not very much.

**9.** Tie in hackles, one or two, depending on feather characteristics, hook size, or desire to have a heavily hackled fly or lightly hackled fly. The hackles are tied in directly in front of the body.

**10.** We're tying the fly here with two hackles, since it's being tied on a relatively large hook and it's being tied heavily hackled for greater floatability in fast water. Grab the first feather with hackle pliers and then wind toward the hook eye.

**11.** Wrap the first hackle with the turns not too close to each other. This will lessen matting down the fibers when the second hackle is wrapped. Secure the hackle with a couple of turns of thread, being careful not to crowd the hook eye.

**12.** Once the first hackle is wound and secured to the hook shank, begin wrapping the second hackle. As in all two-hackled flies, wind the second hackle through the first with a slight back-and-forth weaving motion. You'll find by doing this the fibers from the first hackle won't be matted down.

**13.** Snip off the excess end of the second hackle, then secure with a couple thread wraps.

**14.** Complete the fly head with a couple more thread wraps, covering the two snipped hackle ends. Then throw a whip-finish knot.

**15.** Now is the point where you'll shorten the turkey quill slip by making an oblique cut, with scissors, across the wing. This will result in the top part of the wing being approximately twice the body length. The bottom of the wing is a tad longer.

I like to tie my Kings River Caddis with approximately one-third of the folded turkey feather extending beyond the hook bend. But you can adjust wing length to fit your own preferences. In any case, the wing should extend at least a body-length beyond the hook bend.

**16.** Add a drop of head cement to the fly.

**17.** The completed Kings River Caddis, one of the first effective caddis flies created.

While many of the early caddisfly patterns were first developed in the West, Eastern fly anglers recognized the importance of the natural insect on their home waters. Swarms of American Grannoms bring trout to the surface, especially during egg-laying. Patterns such as the Kings River Caddis are still effective at that time.

# CHAPTER 12

# Llama

## *Streamer*

*"Ray said that on the Wolf River in Wisconsin he had personally only seen two limits of trout taken on this stream, one with worms and the other with this pattern—the Llama."*

*—Eric Leiser, "Tying the Llama Fly and Why,"* Fly Fisherman, *June/July 1973.*

When Groundhog Day comes around on February 2 every year, I sometimes wonder what former fly-tying materials vendor, fly-fishing author, and fly tier Eric Leiser is thinking. It's the day that Punxsutawney Phil, the most celebrated groundhog of all time, emerges from his burrow in southeastern Pennsylvania to see if it's cloudy or sunny. If Phil sees his shadow, folklore tells us that we will have six more weeks of winter.

We've all seen Phil in pictures or footage of his event, being raised to the large crowd of onlookers by a handler wearing a top hat and black frock coat. As cute as the furry critter is, I wonder if Leiser stares at Phil with a different purpose. It wouldn't surprise me if Eric focuses not on the weather forecast but instead on Phil's hair, the perfect material for tying trout flies.

Leiser once wrote that the hair from the back of a groundhog—or woodchuck, as most fly tiers refer to the animal—"is the most desirable piece of fly-tying material I own, other than basic rooster necks." Eric used the banded woodchuck hair for two of his favorite flies, the Chuck Caddis and the Llama. While the Llama isn't original with Eric—he makes that clear in two articles he wrote in the 1970s for *Fly Fisherman*, he's responsible for popularizing the pattern. Miles Tourellot, a Menominee Indian from Wisconsin, originated the pattern.

Fly-tying author Eric Leiser popularized the Llama, one of his favorite patterns. It's an old pattern that goes back to the 1940s. Miles Tourellot, a Menominee Indian from Wisconsin, originated the pattern. It's been said to be as effective as Matuka-style patterns. The woodchuck guard hairs combined with the soft underfur enable the fly to pulsate in the water.

In his June/July 1973 *Fly Fisherman* story titled "Tying the Llama Fly and Why," Eric explained that the pattern had been in existence for at least twenty-five years, making it a 1940s (or earlier) creation. The Llama was sent to Eric by a Wisconsin angler named Ray Benedict who praised its virtues as a top fish-getter on the Wolf River. At first, Eric took what Benedict told him with a grain of salt. But after field-testing it for three years, he concluded that the Llama was indeed everything Benedict reported; it worked well for Eric when other patterns failed him. Leiser sang praises for the Llama and the woodchuck hair that contributes to its effectiveness.

While I'm sure Eric views Punxsutawney Phil with kinder eyes, he's always been on the lookout for woodchuck skins. Now living in Florida, outside of the woodchuck's habitat range, he once asked me if I knew anyone in my area who could provide him with good woodchuck pelts. During the time he was still living in New York State, Eric was known to stop for woodchuck roadkill. For Leiser, a dead woodchuck on a highway was macadam gold.

In *The Founding Flies* I described such an incident when Eric picked up a dead woodchuck he spotted when he was driving along on a road in the Catskill Mountains in New York. There was no way Eric would have driven past the critter that day without stopping to pick it up. The woodchuck hair was just too desirable to leave behind.

In a June 1979 *Fly Fisherman* follow-up story titled "How Many Flies can a Woodchuck . . . ," Eric explained his fascination for the animal's guard hair. The hair is soft yet strong and firm. He liked it for dry flies, like his Chuck Caddis, because he believed the hair floats better and is more durable than deer hair. When using longer hair tufts for streamer flies such as the Llama, the underfur pulsates when retrieved or worked through the current.

The Llama's lively action is the key to its effectiveness. Once Eric trumpeted the pattern in his writings, he began to receive reports from anglers who declared the Llama's effectiveness on par with Matukas and traditional streamers such as the well-known Ghost streamers.

## Fishing the Llama

The Llama is a versatile pattern that can be fished on lakes, ponds, and streams. It's not only a great trout pattern; it's also a great smallmouth bass fly. Fishing the Llama is no different than fishing most any streamer pattern—varying technique depending on water type, conditions, and the species you're after.

Employ the usual streamer fishing techniques during normal conditions on moderate-size trout streams. Understanding fish habitat and holding areas is critical to success. Cross-stream casting to holding areas along undercut stream banks, upstream casting, quarter-upstream casting to get the fly submerged, and quarter-downstream casting are all common streamer fishing methods.

I've used sink-tip lines and even shooting heads when fishing streamers in high water. Those lines are also useful for trolling streamers such as the Llama. Slow-rowing a canoe in S-curves relatively close to a pond or lake shoreline during early spring is a great technique I've used often.

## Tying the Llama

The Llama's primary feature is its three-band woodchuck hair wing. Woodchuck is sold in small patches by fly-tying material supply houses. However, it's best to get your hands on an entire woodchuck pelt. It's important to use the hair that grows on the woodchuck's back as opposed to its belly or sides. Having a complete pelt will ensure you have the correct material. If you're planning on tying large quantities of the pattern—and believe me, you will—it's more cost-effective to purchase an entire hide. However, if you prefer to tie just a few Llamas, make sure you let your material vendor know that you're after woodchuck hair from the back of the animal.

Varmint hunters are a good source for woodchuck, if you're inclined to do your own hide preparation; it's not that difficult. As cute as Punxsutawney Phil might be to some folks, others view the animal as an unwelcome nuisance on farmlands or horse pastures where their burrows and dirt mounds pose hazards to farm equipment and livestock. Hides obtained in the spring of the year are best.

Besides the hair, hook choice often surfaces when discussion turns to tying Llamas. Eric tied his first Llamas on the once-popular Mustad 38941 hook. But as Eric noted, there's a variety of hook models that serve tying the Llama well. He also made the point that the hair length found on the particular patch or hide that you purchased will help determine the hook model you need. Some streamer hook models have longer shanks than others. As Eric said, "you match the hook to the guard hairs." Guard hair length varies from animal to animal.

The tying steps that follow represent the most common version of the Llama, tied with a red floss body. You can also tie the pattern with black, white, yellow or other floss colors. The woodchuck wing is the feature that remains constant between the many Llama color combinations. White, black and yellow Llamas are typically ribbed with silver tinsel instead of gold. While gold tinsel was used on original red floss body Llamas, I prefer silver tinsel on all of my Llama patterns. I'm showing the pattern tied with flat silver tinsel here, but use the original gold tinsel if that is your preference. I use metal tinsel on the floss streamer body ribbing because Mylar tinsel has a tendency to slip and move once wrapped up the floss body. However, if Mylar tinsel is your material of choice, then use it. An advantage of Mylar is that it's less expensive than metal tinsel.

There are many different variations of the Llama, the common factor being the woodchuck guard hair wing. Red Llamas are usually tied with gold tinsel ribbing, as used in the original pattern, but silver works well, too. The yellow, black, and white Llamas are usually ribbed with silver tinsel.

Many streamer fly tiers prefer small heads on their flies, something they even strive for, mainly from an artistic or aesthetic reason. However, you'll want to build up your thread head on the Llama so that there's enough area to accommodate the painted white eye and black pupil. It's difficult to paint the round eyes on small heads.

## DRESSING

| | |
|---|---|
| **Hook:** | Mustad 3665A, 79580 |
| **Thread:** | Black 6/0 UNI-Thread |
| **Tail:** | Grizzly hackle fibers (soft) |
| **Rib:** | Lagartun flat silver tinsel |
| **Body:** | Danville Red floss, four-strand |
| **Wing:** | Woodchuck hair from back of animal, guard hair, and underfur |
| **Hackle:** | Grizzly |
| **Head:** | White enamel paint eye and black enamel paint pupil |

**Note:** The original design used flat gold tinsel for the rib.

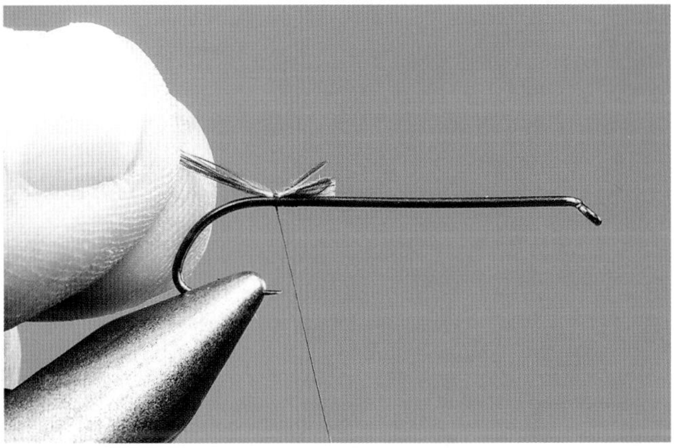

**1.** Tie on thread at hook bend then attach grizzly hackle barbs. The fibers should be webby, soft, and approximately one and a half times the hook gap in length.

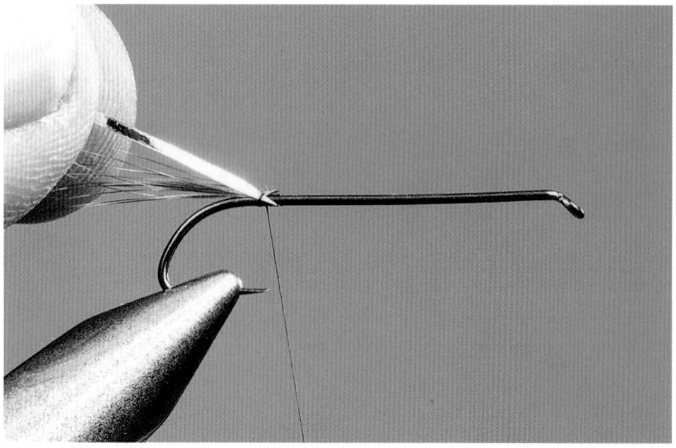

**2.** Taper the end of medium silver tinsel and attach at the tail position. (Use gold tinsel if preferred.)

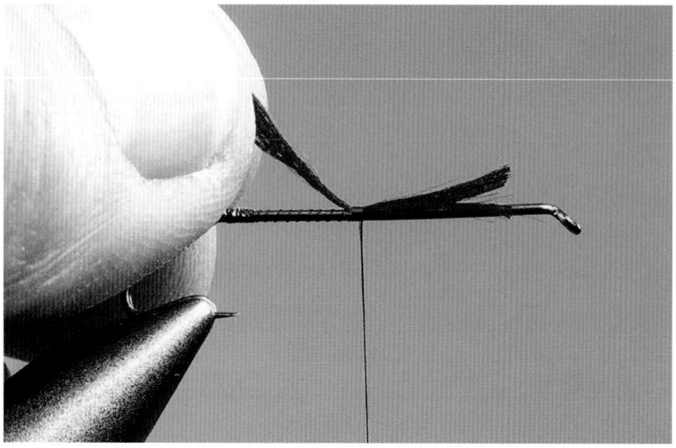

**3.** Attach four-stranded red floss to the hook shank midpoint. Attaching the floss at the midpoint will enable the formation of a tapered body.

**4.** Wrap the floss to a point just short of the hook eye, then secure the material with three winds of thread. The thread will remain in this position, ready to accept the floss on its return trip.

**5.** Wrap the floss back down to the hook bend then back up the hook shank to where your thread is waiting. Secure the floss with additional thread wraps and then snip off the excess material. The body is now ready to accept the tinsel ribbing.

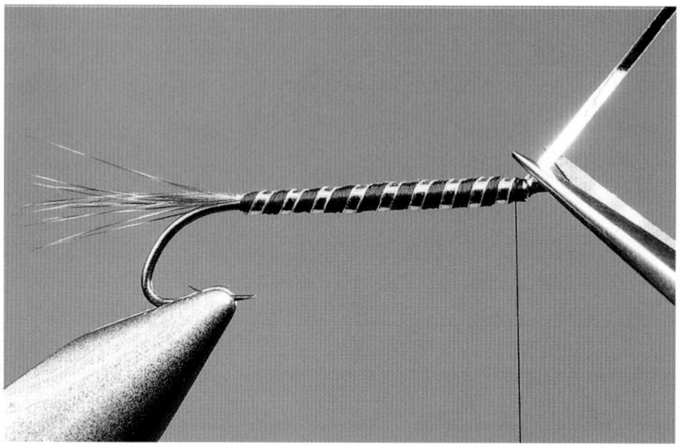

**6.** Wind the tinsel forward along the floss body with even wraps. Secure the tinsel with three thread wraps once it reaches its end position up near the hook eye. Important: use caution in securing the tinsel with the thread. The metal tinsel's sharp edges can easily sever the thread. Make sure to not crowd the hook eye area. You're going to need hook shank space once the woodchuck hair is attached. You'll also need space to form a nice thread head.

**7.** Woodchuck fur is a versatile material, especially the three-banded feature of the guard hair like you see in this photo. Snip off a swath of hair, close to the base, that includes the soft underfur as well as the guard hairs.

**8.** Tie in the swath of woodchuck hair where the floss body and ribbing ended. Snip off the excess hair.

**9.** Select a soft, webby grizzly hackle and tie in at the wing base.

**10.** Move the tying thread to a point just behind the hook eye, and wrap forward two or three turns of the grizzly hackle.

**11.** Secure the last turn of hackle to the hook shank with two or three thread wraps.

**12.** Gently grasp the hackle barb fibers with your thumb and index finger and pull back, being careful not to disturb the tinsel ribbing. The goal is to flare the hackle fibers back a bit. If you're using Mylar tinsel, the nice, neatly spaced ribbing you've created can easily slip out of place along the floss while manipulating the hackle fibers.

**13.** I like my Llamas with a good-size head. Build up the head with thread so that it's ready to accept the painted eyes. Throw a whip-finish knot.

**14.** Add several coats of cement or glossy varnish to the head. Let each coat dry well, preferably overnight. You want a nice, smooth head surface ready to accept the painted eyes.

**15.** Add a drop of white enamel to the head. It's best to remove the fly from the vise and place on your tying table for this procedure. You can make the white circle by snipping off the end of a round toothpick with a single edge razor blade and using the cut end as a stamp. Let the white paint dry overnight before adding the black pupil.

**16.** Cut off the end of another toothpick, but just a tiny amount this time. You want the black pupil, painted with a small drop of enamel, to be a smaller diameter than the white eye. Let it dry overnight, and your Llama is completed.

# CHAPTER 13

# Male Dace

## *Streamer*

*"Of course many anglers do not use streamers in low clear water but I find these effective."*

*—Lew Oatman, letter to Joseph Bates Jr., 1958*

Lew Oatman died in April 1958 during the time he was still corresponding with Joe Bates concerning his streamer patterns that would be included in the now classic book Bates was writing, *Streamer Fly Tying and Fishing* (1966). Many of the details concerning the interactions between Oatman and Bates are described in *The Founding Flies*, along with photographs of Oatman-tied streamers. Keith Fulsher, Lew's contemporary and friend, contributed to Bates's *Streamer Fly Tying and Fishing* by tying several streamer patterns that Bates was unable to acquire directly from Oatman. One of several Oatman-designed patterns tied by Keith that appears in Bates's book is the Male Dace.

It was Bates's book that raised Oatman's profile as a pioneer in streamer fly design. In his book *Trout* (1978), Ernie Schwiebert said that Oatman tied his streamers "so beautifully that they were as exquisite as the most elegant dry flies of the Catskill School."

Oatman's Male Dace is indeed a nice-looking imitation of the minnow it represents, the male blacknose dace in its spawning colors. A common minnow that inhabits flowing water, the blacknose dace (*Rhinichthys atratulus*) spawns in May or June, during which time the males develop a rusty orange or red stripe below the characteristic black side stripe. Badger hackle, with

**The blacknose dace spawns in May or June, during which time the males develop a rusty orange or red stripe below the characteristic black side stripe. Badger hackle, with its dark black center, suggests the minnow's black stripe that runs from the head to tail, while the orange hackle fiber throat suggests the minnow's spawning color.**

Lew Oatman at his tying bench in Shushan, New York. Fly-fishing author Ernie Schwiebert called Oatman,"the father of the scientific approach to baitfish patterns."This photo was shot by Herb Eriksson in the mid-1950s. HERB ERIKSSON

The male blacknose dace minnow exhibits distinctive orange or red colorations as spring breeding season approaches. Lew Oatman tied his Male Dace with rusty orange hackle fibers at the throat to simulate the minnow's orange pectoral fins, as shown here.

its dark black center, suggests the minnow's black stripe that runs from the head to tail. Oatman used orange hackle barb fibers in his Male Dace streamer to suggest the male blacknose dace's breeding colors.

## Fishing the Male Dace

As is the case with all Oatman's streamer patterns, the Male Dace can be fished in a variety of water types for a variety of gamefish. Keith Fulsher provided me with a copy of the complete, original letter that Lew Oatman wrote to Bates, excerpts of which appeared in *Streamer Fly Tying and Fishing*. Oatman indicated that he fished streamers in all water types and under many stream conditions, including in low, clear water as well as high, turbulent water.

As might be expected, he varied fishing technique and pattern selection relative to the type of water he was fishing. He said that when fishing medium-depth water, deep pockets, or turbulent currents, a larger-size streamer should be fished with "violent action given to it or even a slap-cast to attract attention." Quieter, shallower waters should be fished with patterns that are tied sparsely and "the action given it should be gentler."

The Male Dace streamer is a useful pattern, coast to coast and in many waters not inhabited by the minnow it was meant to resemble. While Oatman intended that the pattern be fished to imitate the common blacknose dace minnow, a species found throughout the Great Lakes and Mississippi watersheds, its form and flash can suggest many other baitfish, or even some juvenile fish.

## Tying the Male Dace

Lew Oatman's patterns are often designed with two different saddle hackle shades used for crafting the wings. Nesting golden badger saddle hackles over each side of two dyed olive saddle hackles creates the Male Dace wings. It may take a couple attempts to get all four hackles positioned correctly. The pattern is relatively easy to tie, other than the minor frustrations you may experience getting the hackles positioned together so that they don't splay out from each other.

### DRESSING

| | |
|---|---|
| **Hook:** | #4-12 Mustad 3665A |
| **Thread:** | Black UNI-Thread |
| **Rib:** | Lagartun flat gold tinsel |
| **Body:** | Danville Cream floss, four-strand |
| **Throat:** | Orange hackle fibers |
| **Wing:** | Two golden badger saddle hackles and two olive green saddle hackles |
| **Cheeks:** | Jungle cock eyes (small) |

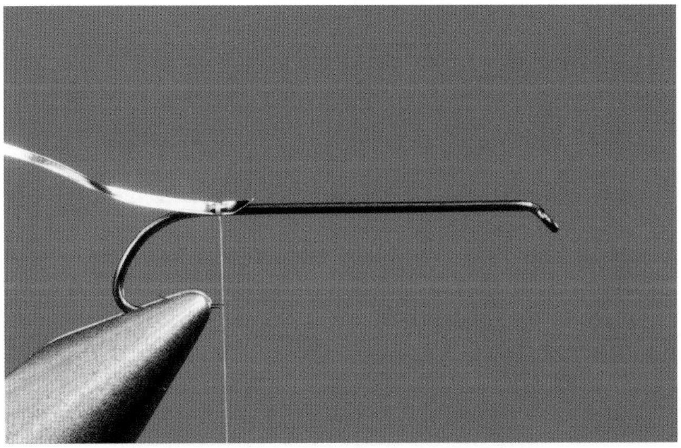

**1.** Attach white thread at hook bend, directly above the hook point. Secure approximately 8 inches of medium flat gold tinsel with a couple thread wraps. You can adjust the tinsel working length based on the hook size and model. White thread is used for the first few steps so that black thread, which will be used later for the fly head, doesn't show through the cream-shade floss.

**2.** Wind the white tying thread forward, with close wraps, to the hook shank midpoint. For a size 12 Mustad 3665A hook as shown here, attach approximately 10 inches of cream-shade four-strand floss at the midpoint. The working length of floss you'll need will vary with hook size and model. Extend the floss end forward to a distance that will equal the total body length.

**3.** Continue binding the floss with tight, close thread wraps to its forward end.

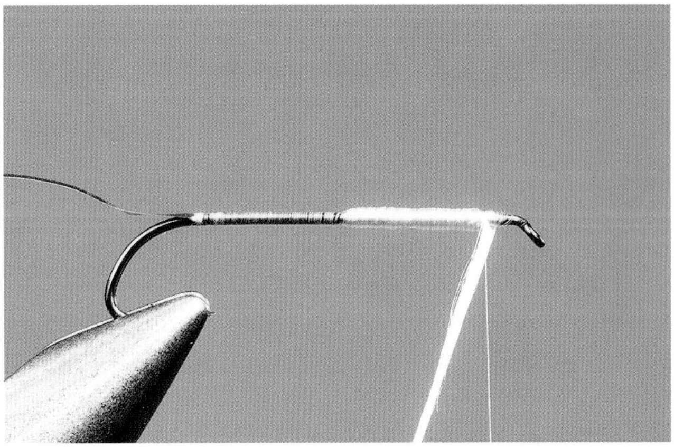

**4.** Begin building the tapered body by wrapping the four-strand floss forward, then securing with two thread wraps at a point set back from the hook eye a distance that will allow room for the fly head.

**5.** Wrap the floss back to the hook bend, reverse direction, and wrap back to the fly head position. Secure with a couple turns of thread.

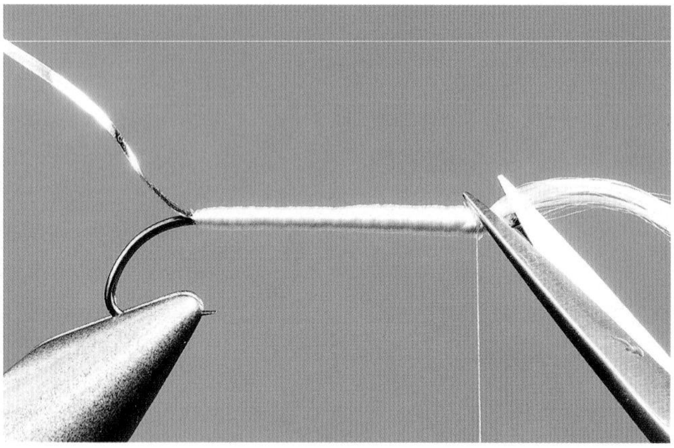

**6.** Snip the end of excess floss.

**7.** Bring forward the flat, medium gold tinsel that has been waiting patiently at the hook bend with even wraps around the floss body. Secure it at its front end with a couple of thread wraps. Caution: if you're using metal tinsel, make sure the sharp edge doesn't cut the tying thread.

**8.** Select a webby, dyed orange feather for the streamer's throat.

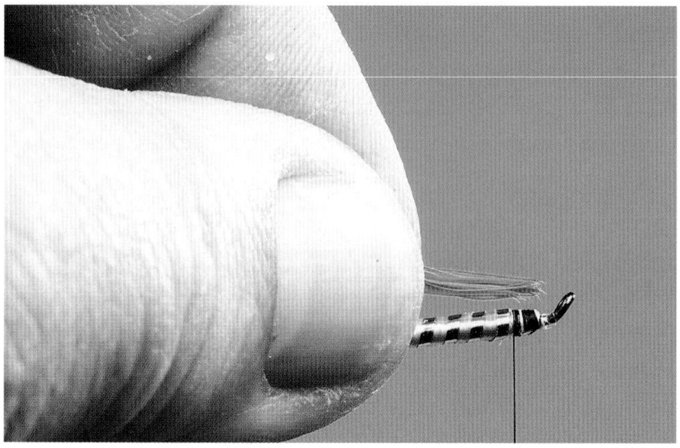

**9.** Remove fly from vise, turn upside down, then return fly to vise. Or, if you use a rotating vise, rotate the fly to an upside-down position. Tie off the white thread, snip the end, then start black thread in the same position. Remove a small tuft of the orange hackle barb fibers from the feather and position the tuft over the hook for attachment.

**10.** Attach webby orange hackle fibers to the underside of the fly. The length of the fibers should be about one to one and a half times the hook gap.

**11.** Select two golden badger saddle hackles and two olive-dyed saddle hackles. The streamer wing is built by nesting the two olive saddle hackles inside the two badger saddle hackles.

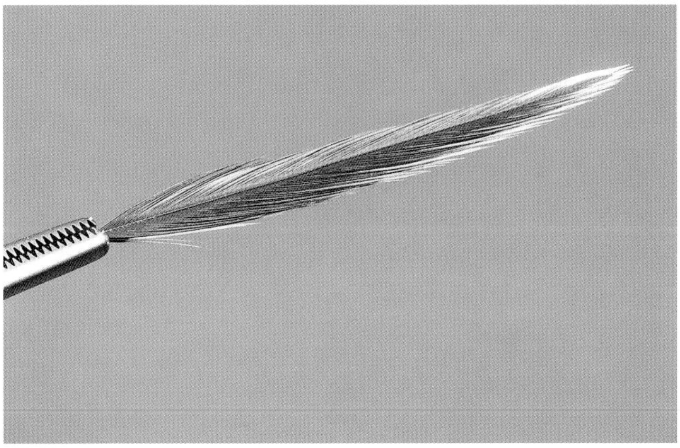

**12.** Nest the olive saddle hackle underneath the badger hackle, forming one side of the wing. This is how the two feathers, for one side of the wing, would appear.

**13.** This is how the two feathers of one side of the wing would appear from the outside. The olive saddle hackle is under the badger, creating one side of the wing.

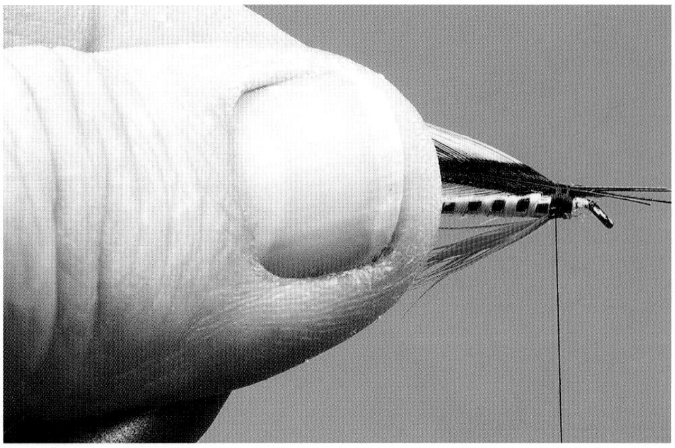

**14.** Gather the four saddle hackle feathers—two badger, two olive. Tie the four feathers down on top of the hook shank. Two olive saddle hackles are placed against each other, concave side (dull side) to concave side. The two badger saddle hackles surround the two olive saddle hackles, concave sides against the olive saddles. In other words, the far wing pair cups in against the close wing pair. The saddle ends should extend about the length of the hook gap beyond the hook bend.

**15.** Snip off the excess saddle hackle quill stems.

**16.** Select a small jungle cock eye and secure along the side of the head area.

**17.** Build the head with a number of thread turns. Secure the head with a whip-finish knot. Then snip off the thread.

**18.** Add two or three coats of head cement.

**19.** The Male Dace is completed.

CHAPTER 14

# Martinez Black

## *Nymph*

*"When it comes to wet flies, if I had to, I could get along very nicely with just two patterns—the black wooly worm and the rough-bodied black nymph."*

—*Ray Bergman,* With Fly, Plug, and Bait, *(1947)*

Ray Bergman wrote in *With Fly, Plug, and Bait* about Don Martinez's Martinez Black nymph, a pattern that has been tweaked and changed over the years but has always been known for its shaggy body. Bergman reported that Martinez tied the pattern using dog or wolf fur, dyed black.

The Don Martinez chapter of *The Founding Flies* describes patterns he developed or popularized; the well-known common black Woolly Worm among them. George Grant, the Western woven-body nymph expert called Martinez a "Western dry fly master." Grant credited Martinez for bringing to West Yellowstone, and possibly the entire state of Montana, "real knowledge of how to tie and fish dry flies."

Yet Don Martinez, who died in 1955, also left a legacy in sinking flies, one of the most effective being the Martinez Black. Other fly anglers besides Ray Bergman promoted the nymph. Author A. J. McClane, who knew Martinez from his interactions with him at Yellowstone, listed the Black Martinez in both his *Practical Fly Fisherman* (1951) and *Standard Fishing Encyclopedia* (1965). The pattern also gained exposure in fly-fishing and fly-tying supply house catalogs. The Martinez Black was a favorite of Visalia, California, shop owner Buz Buszek. Don Lieb, who in

Don Martinez, who died in 1955, left a legacy in the flies he developed during his years in West Yellowstone. Many were dry flies, yet one of his most effective patterns was a sinker—the Martinez Black nymph. Fishing author A. J. McClane helped raise the profile of the pattern. It soon became a favorite of fly shops, such as Buz Buszek's in Visalia, California.

While Don Martinez was influenced by East Coast Catskill tiers, his patterns were developed for West Coast rivers such as the Yellowstone. Patterns such as his Black Martinez filled bins at his West Yellowstone fly shop.

the 1960s tied flies for Buz, tied the Martinez Black that appears in *The Founding Flies*.

My first exposure to the Martinez Black came through *McClane's Standard Fishing Encyclopedia*. Catskill-region fly tier Elsie Darbee tied an example of the pattern that appeared in McClane's color plates. Elsie's flies that appeared in McClane served as my primary fly pattern reference during my teenage years. It's an easy fly for a kid or beginner to tackle.

## Fishing the Martinez Black

From as far back as I can remember, the "old-timers" have insisted that it's best to fish a dark black fly pattern during turbid water conditions. There was always an insistence that black patterns—such as the classic Black Gnat or Black Prince wet flies—were best during late-night fishing. Black casts a silhouette more easily detected by fish. I've never fished the Martinez Black at night since I've grown accustomed to using a large Black Prince, which has served me well and which I know is effective. (I expect to leave my comfort zone and try a Black Martinez the next time I'm fishing at night). But cloudy water conditions bring a Black Martinez out of my fly box. However, the Black Martinez can be fished most anytime and under most any water conditions.

## Tying the Martinez Black

Besides the black dog or wolf fur that Ray Bergman reported in his 1947 book, seal fur dyed black was also used for the fly body. Elsie Darbee listed black seal as the body material for the pattern. Dyed seal is still available; salmon fly tiers frequently use the material. However, there are a couple of acceptable substitute materials that can be used for body dubbing.

Friends of mine who used seal fur in the past have experienced good results with dyed opossum fur. It has nice translucency, similar to seal fur, and isn't overly expensive. I've used it myself on other fly patterns that originally called for seal fur. The third choice is common dyed black wool yarn.

Wool doesn't have the sheen that seal or opossum provides, but it's still a good substitute. It's best to blend pieces into a loose dubbing rather than simply wrapping a stand on the hook shank; you'll end up with a much buggier-looking fly.

I've selected oval gold tinsel for the Martinez Black version demonstrated here. Early versions of the pattern used copper wire. I've demonstrated the pattern using tinsel, just as Don Lieb selected for his example that he tied to include in *The Founding Flies*, but copper wire is acceptable.

The wing case is created with dyed raffia grass. Raffia was a popular fly-tying material used in everything from nymphs to extended dry-fly bodies. It's strong, easy to work with, and inexpensive. You can purchase small bundles of raffia from fabric supply stores or craft stores. One small bundle will last a lifetime. My supply is natural straw color but dyed raffia is also available. One method to arrive at the green shade required for the Martinez Black case is to dye a small section with a green indelible ink pen.

The tail material used here is guinea hen fibers, a common, inexpensive fly-tying material. Early pattern versions used peacock sword feather fibers, but guinea is now more common as a tail material for the Martinez Black.

## DRESSING

| | |
|---|---|
| **Hook:** | #8-12 Mustad 9671 |
| **Thread:** | Black 6/0 UNI-Thread |
| **Tail:** | Speckled guinea hen body feather fibers |
| **Rib:** | Lagartun oval gold tinsel or copper wire |
| **Body:** | Black seal fur, dyed black angora goat fur, dyed black opossum, or dyed black lamb's wool |
| **Wing Case:** | Dyed green raffia grass |
| **Thorax:** | Black chenille |
| **Hackle:** | Gray partridge |

**1.** Select a guinea hen feather and snip off a few fibers for tailing.

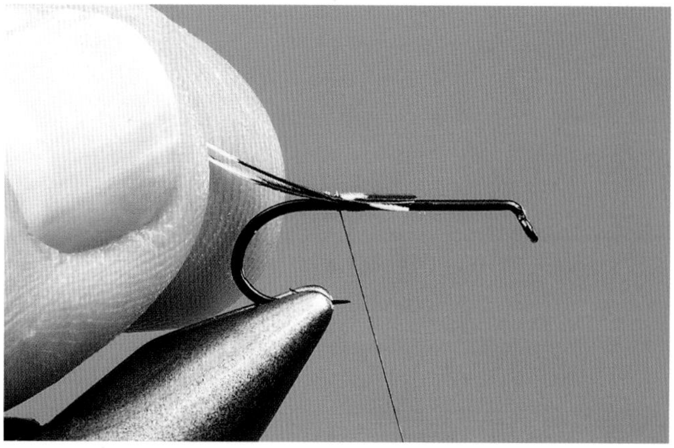

**2.** Tie thread at hook bend. Attach a few guinea hen fibers on the shank above the hook point.

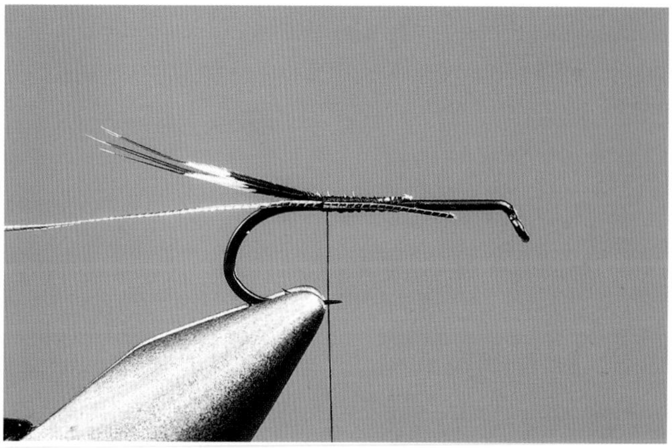

**3.** At the tail position, attach a length of oval gold tinsel.

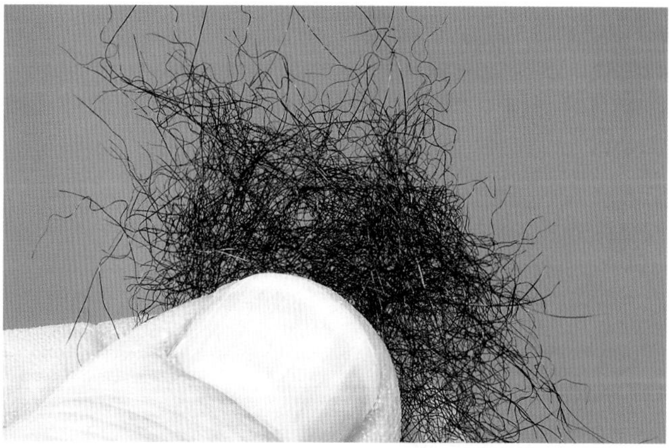

**4.** Gather a small amount of dyed black seal fur dubbing or similar material such as lamb's wool, angora goat fur dyed black or opossum fur dyed black. If you're using wool, cut a length of yarn into one-inch pieces. Create dubbing by mixing the pieces in a blender for a minute or two. You'll end up with a much fuzzier and buggy-looking fly body than simply wrapping a strand of yarn on the hook shank.

**5.** Attach black dubbing to thread using your method of choice. Seal and opossum can be difficult to attach to the thread. If you're using one of these materials, lay the dubbing loosely onto the thread. Pinch and roll the material counterclockwise with more force than you would normally use. You can also run tying wax along the thread to help the material adhere more tenaciously.

**6.** Wind the black body dubbing forward about three-fourths the hook shank length.

**7.** Grasp the oval gold tinsel and then spiral it up the body three or four turns to form the fly ribbing. Secure the end of the tinsel with a couple tying thread wraps, then snip off the remaining excess tinsel.

**8.** Attach a section of dyed green raffia grass at the front end of the black fur body. This will form the wing case.

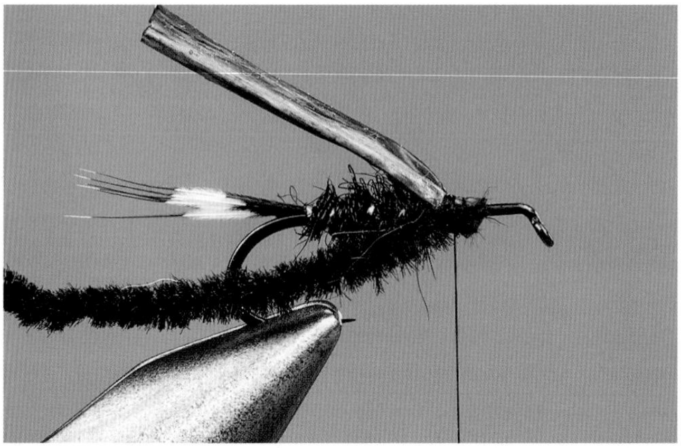

**9.** Attach a length of black chenille at a point directly in front of the body. This will form the nymph thorax.

**10.** Wind the chenille to a point just behind the hook eye, being careful to not crowd the eye. Snip off the excess chenille.

**11.** Pull the section of raffia firmly forward over the black chenille, then secure with tying thread near the hook eye.

**12.** Tie in a small partridge hackle directly in front of the raffia wing case.

**13.** Grasp the end of the partridge hackle, then wind forward a couple of turns.

**14.** Secure the hackle with thread and then snip off the excess.

**15.** The partridge hackle is flared to the rear by gently pulling back the fibers. Make two or three tying thread wraps to secure the fibers in place.

**16.** Build a small head with tying thread then throw a whip-finish knot to complete the fly.

**17.** The completed Martinez Black nymph, still a great trout-taker.

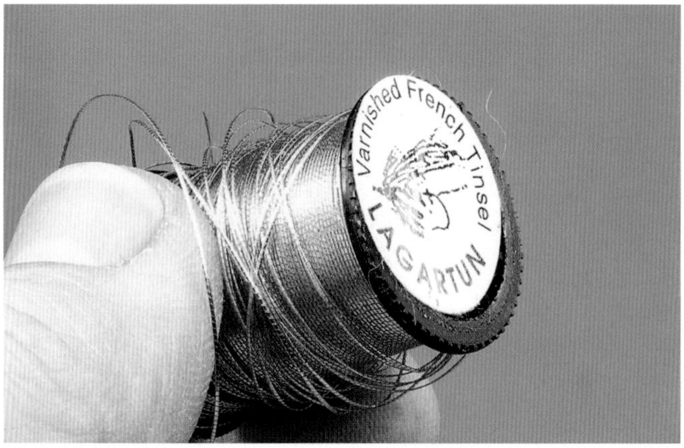


Lagartun brand oval gold tinsel is used for the Martinez Black body ribbing.

Brook trout love colorful flies, but they are also fond of black flies. They love the Martinez Black nymph.

CHAPTER 15

# Michigan Stone

## *Dry fly*

*"We first learned of the pattern some fifteen years ago while fishing the Au Sable River with Mr. Young and his wife, Martha. We were so impressed by its effectiveness when* Isoperla *was over the water that we brought it back to try on Pennsylvania waters."*

—*Chauncy Lively, "The Michigan Stone,"* Pennsylvania Angler, *February 1971*

The "Mr. Young" that Chauncy Lively referred to in his *Pennsylvania Angler* article "The Michigan Stone" is Paul H. Young, the Michigan fly rod builder who died in 1960. Chauncy and his fly-fishing companion, wife Marion, became close friends with Paul and Martha, fishing and visiting with them in Michigan.

After reading about Young's fine cane rods in a *Field & Stream* magazine advertisement, Chauncy contacted Young in 1949 about acquiring a new rod for Marion. From that correspondence came a new 7.5-foot, 3-ounce dry-fly rod. The friendship blossomed over the years, and the two men exchanged numerous letters and began fishing together on favorite trout waters, particularly Michigan's Au Sable River. They obviously discussed fly patterns, Young's Michigan Stone among no doubt many others.

Lively was introduced to the Michigan Stone twenty-five years before his 1971 *Pennsylvania Angler* article was written. That puts the pattern's birth at least as early as the mid-1950s, if not earlier. The pattern is yet another example of a terrific dry fly that has fallen under the radar.

**The Michigan Stone, created by the great rod builder Paul Young and popularized by Chauncy Lively, is not restricted to *Isoperla bilineata*, a common East Coast species often encountered at dusk during June or July when the adult females are over water laying eggs.**

## Fishing the Michigan Stone

The Michigan Stone is not restricted to *Isoperla bilineata*, a common East Coast species often encountered at dusk during June or July when the adult females are over the water laying eggs. The crepuscular activity of egg-laying females signals that it's time to direct attention to fishing *Isoperla bilineata* dry-fly imitations, such as the Michigan Stone. The Michigan Stone would no doubt prove beneficial on Eastern or Western waters inhabited by other *Isoperla* or *Alloperla* species.

The little green *Alloperla* stoneflies can be imitated with a variation of the standard Michigan Stone. However, the Michigan Stone is also a great general attractor pattern; its usefulness goes beyond the Michigan Stone's original intent to imitate emergences of *Isoperla*, known to many fly anglers as the Yellow Sally. You can fish it along riffles, as its buggy look entices fish regardless of twilight stonefly activity.

## Tying the Michigan Stone

I like to tie the Michigan Stone using the Mustad 94842 up-eye dry-fly hook. Lively tied the pattern on both up-eye and down-eye fine wire dry-fly hooks. Use your favorite dry-fly hook model. The Michigan Stone is tied on fairly small hook sizes-size 16 and size 18. If tying the pattern for some *Alloperla* stoneflies, Lively recommended tweaking the general Michigan Stone pattern. Change the hackle to a yellowish-olive shade and use dubbing material that is dyed chartreuse.

### DRESSING

| | |
|---|---|
| **Hook:** | #16-18 Mustad 94842 |
| **Thread:** | Light yellow 8/0 UNI-Thread |
| **Hackle:** | Grizzly |
| **Body:** | Yellow dyed arctic fox or rabbit fur |
| **Wing:** | Deer body hair (fine) |

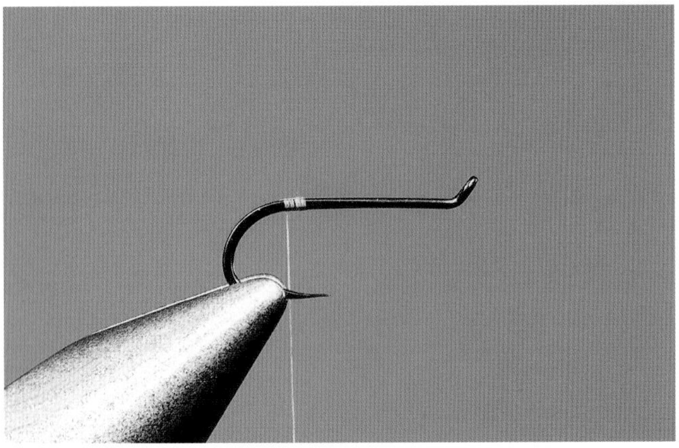

**1.** Begin yellow tying thread at the hook bend on the shank above the hook barb.

**2.** Select two grizzly hackles matched to the hook size. The hackle barb size on the rear of the fly should be one and a half times the hook gap. The front hackle barb length, by design, is slightly shorter than that. Tie in the first hackle at the hook bend.

**3.** Wind the rear hackle four or five turns up the hook shank to a position just past the hook point.

**4.** Snip the excess hackle.

**5.** Attach the yellow dubbing to tying thread. My preference is dyed arctic fox fur, but use your dubbing of choice. Arctic fox has a nice texture for small dry flies.

**6.** The dubbing is wrapped just beyond the hook shank midpoint.

**7.** Cut a swath of fine deer hair, such as coastal deer hair, and place in your hair stacker to even up the tips.

**8.** Tie in the deer hair directly in front of the yellow body. The hair should extend to the rear just beyond the hook bend or no longer than the width of the hook gap.

**9.** Snip off the excess hair butts and secure with a couple thread wraps.

**10.** Tie in the second grizzly hackle, with barb lengths slightly shorter than the rear hackle, in front of the wing.

**11.** Wrap second grizzly hackle two or three turns.

**12.** Snip the excess remaining hackle and then secure with a couple thread wraps.

**13.** Throw a whip-finish knot to complete the fly.

**14.** Add a drop of head cement.

**15.** The Completed Michigan Stone, a great little dry fly that floats well and can attract many fine trout as both an imitator and attractor pattern.

CHAPTER 16

# Missoulian Spook

## *Streamer*

*"The name caught on like wildfire, as did the fly itself, and today every trout fisherman in the West swears by the Missoulian Spook."*

—*Joe Brooks, "Best All-Round Trout Fly,"* Outdoor Life, *October 1963*

The Missoulian Spook was originally called a White Muddler, a spin-off of Don Gapen's well-known Muddler Minnow that proved extremely effective on Western waters. Dan Bailey in Livingston, Montana, created the pattern, a hybrid between the Muddler and an early East Coast fly called the Bumblepuppy.

Theodore Gordon, the assumed father of dry-fly fishing in America, created the Bumblepuppy in the late 1800s. It's a garish, gaudy, almost fanciful pattern tied in many variations by both Gordon himself and his followers in the Catskill region of New York State.

The Theodore Gordon chapter in *The Founding Flies* describes in detail the history of the pattern along with several photos of Bumblepuppy variations. In his writings, Gordon sang the praises of the fly; he found it effective for bass, bream, rockfish, perch, sunfish, pike, salmon, striped bass, pickerel, and big trout that fed on minnows. He had hoped to take a muskellunge on a Bumblepuppy. The pattern might not have captured a big muskie as Gordon hoped, but it did take a 13-pound Catskill-region brown trout at the mouth of the Mongaup River, in the Delaware River. The fish was a record that year in the *Field & Stream* fishing contest.

**The Missoulian Spook was originally called a White Muddler, a spin-off of Don Gapen's well-known Muddler Minnow that proved extremely effective on Western waters. Dan Bailey, in Livingston, Montana, created the pattern, a hybrid between the Muddler and an early East Coast fly called the Bumblepuppy.**

The mouth of Salmon Creek, Cayuga Lake, several miles from Ithaca, New York, offered interesting early- and late-season Muddler fly-fishing sessions, thanks to the gravel bar that extends out into the lake. The creek enters the lake from the left of the photo, spilling gravel and sediment at its mouth. Modern-style White Muddlers were effective for taking silver-bullet lake rainbows just after sunrise, in late fall, by wading out into the lake along the bar. White Muddlers evolved into a simple style that lack many of the features found on the Missoulian Spook "White Muddlers."

Bailey, a Catskill-vicinity resident who later relocated to Livingston, Montana, was aware of Gordon's Bumblepuppy. He also helped popularize the Muddler Minnow, Don Gapen's 1936 creation that was responsible for taking many large trout on his Western waters. The Don Gapen chapter in *The Founding Flies* explains the details that led to the Muddler Minnow's creation.

Bailey was fishing one day, cogitating trout flies and potential adaptations. Knowledge of Gordon's Bumblepuppy and Gapen's Muddler inspired him to mate the two patterns, resulting in the White Muddler. Bumblepuppy influences are found in the White Muddler's red chenille butt tag, white body and silver tinsel ribbing. Muddler influences are found in the White Muddler's deer hair collar and clipped deer hair head. Some versions of the Bumblepuppy (there are many) used mottled turkey quill slips for the wings, as is true with the Muddler.

Fly anglers embraced the hybrid pattern but one fly fisher named V. T. Hamlin (the *T*, incidentally, stood for *Trout*) decided to alter its name from White Muddler to Missoulian Spook. Hamlin was the creator of the long-running syndicated *Alley Oop* comic strip. The October 24, 1956 strip illustrated a jumping trout with a large White Muddler hanging from its mouth. The fly name stuck and from that point forward creation was labeled a Missoulian Spook.

## Fishing The Missoulian Spook

In his *Outdoor Life* article, Brooks wrote that the Missoulian Spook could be fished in a variety of ways but was most effective for him fished on top the water surface. He believed that the Missoulian Spook outperformed the Muddler when fished in that manner. However, Brooks believed that the Muddler still surpassed the Missoulian Spook's overall effectiveness. Brooks quoted Bailey's comment: "The Missoulian Spook, or White Muddler, is terrific, but it doesn't approach the original Muddler Minnow."

There was a time that Dan Bailey's fly shop tied and sold Missoulian Spook patterns in numbers. In years past, Bailey's shop stapled flies like Muddlers and Missoulian Spook patterns to small Bailey's fly shop cards. There's one pictured in *The Founding Flies*, from my own collection.

The Missoulian Spook was never among the Muddler variations that I once tied and fished. But I do intend to fish it in the coming season on my home Battenkill River waters. In recent years, I've drifted away from routinely fishing Muddlers or even contemporary White Muddlers, but I still have boxes of them that occasionally find their way into my fishing vest.

During the height of my Muddler years—in the late 1970s—I fished them primarily during late fall and early spring at the mouth of Salmon Creek, a small tributary running into Cayuga Lake in the finger lakes country of New York State. I used to wade out on a gravel bar off the mouth, as far as possible into the lake, then cast "pure white" White Muddlers (not the Spook) and regular Muddlers as far as possible using crude, homemade shooting heads. The silver-bullet rainbows that came in close to shore that time of year hammered the White Muddler. I wonder if the Missoulian Spook would have also taken fish. It probably would have.

## DRESSING

| | |
|---|---|
| **Hook:** | #6-12 Mustad 9672 |
| **Thread:** | White 6/0 UNI-Thread |
| **Tail:** | Light-colored mottled turkey quill slip |
| **Tag:** | Red chenille |
| **Rib:** | Lagartun silver tinsel (medium) |
| **Body:** | White wool |
| **Underwing:** | A few fibers from barred teal flank feather |
| **Wing:** | Light (almost pure white) mottled turkey quill slip |
| **Collar:** | Pale tan deer body hair or white calf tail underwing |
| **Head:** | White deer body hair |

**1.** Attach thread to the hook bend area. Snip off a small section of very light—almost white—mottled turkey quill. Secure the small feather slip at the hook bend to form the tail. The tail length, once completed, should be approximately the width of the hook gap.

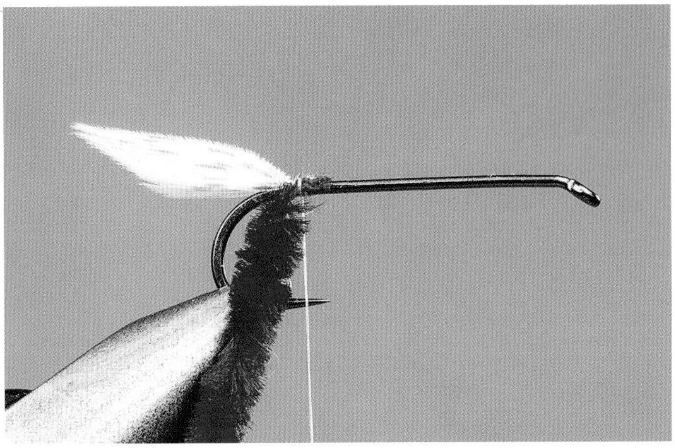

**2.** Attach approximately 3 inches of red chenille directly in front of the tail. The best way to attach chenille to the hook is to strip away some of the fuzzy material from the string, leaving a bare spot that's easily secured to the hook shank.

**3.** Make one or two wraps of the chenille, then secure with two thread wraps. Snip off the remaining excess material. The fly butt is now completed.

**4.** Secure a length of silver tinsel directly in front of the red chenille butt.

**5.** Secure a length of white yarn also directly in front of the red chenille butt. Move the thread forward up the hook shank to a position ready to accept the white yarn and the silver tinsel ribbing.

**6.** Wrap the white yarn up approximately two-thirds of the hook shank length. Secure with two thread wraps and then snip off the excess.

**7.** Grab the silver tinsel that has been waiting patiently to be wrapped forward to create the fly's ribbing. Make several evenly spaced wraps over the wool. Secure with thread once it reaches the end of the body. Be careful if you're using Lagartun metal tinsel. The sharp edges can quickly sever your thread. There's nothing more discouraging than to watch your tinsel ribbing unravel, along with the thread. The thread continues to hang in the same position, ready to accept the wings.

**8.** Select a few fibers from a teal flank feather. You want straight fibers of even length.

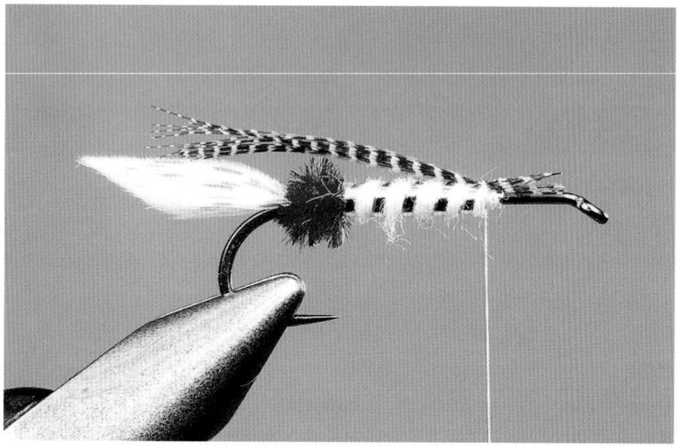

**9.** Secure the teal flank feather fibers to the hook shank. The lengths should extend to the rear, halfway across the top of the turkey quill section tail.

**10.** Select two mottled turkey wing quills, one from a right wing, one from a left wing. The quills should have sections that are very light, almost white, with faint mottles. Snip a section from each wing quill. The width of each section should be about the length of the hook gap, maybe a tad wider.

**11.** Place one turkey quill slip on top of the other, concave sides (dull sides) against each other. The slip lengths should extend to the rear halfway across the tail, as shown. Hold the two quill slips together with your thumb and index finger and position above the hook shank. With a couple thread wraps, secure the wings firmly to the hook shank, being careful to make sure that they are dead center on top of the teal flank feather fibers. Snip off the excess wing butts.

**12.** You'll need two deer body hair shades. The natural shade will be used to create the small, flared collar. The white hair will be used to form the clipped head.

**13.** Place a small quantity of fine-hair, natural shade deer hair into your stacker and even up the tips.

**14.** Position the swath of stacked natural shade deer hair at a point directly in front of the wing with the hair extending to the rear, halfway across the white yarn/silver ribbed body. As you're securing the hair to the hook, let some of the hairs rotate around the entire fly. Snip off the remaining hair butts, being careful not to snip your thread in the process.

**15.** Cut off a swath of the white deer body hair (it need not be stacked), and spin it around the hook shank. You'll add several hair swath increments, spinning the hair around the hook shank and compacting each increment tightly against the last.

**16.** After adding a few white hair increments, enough to complete a full head, tie off with a whip-finish knot.

The Missoulian Spook was first popularized on Western Rivers, such as the Big Hole in Montana.

**17.** Clip off the white deer hair into a neat head.

**18.** Add a drop of head cement to the fly.

**19.** The completed Missoulian Spook, a great Muddler-style pattern and a cousin of an old pattern called the Bumble-puppy.

CHAPTER 17

# Shushan Postmaster

## *Streamer*

*"The Shushan Postmaster bucktail is a fine one for brook and brown trout in the United States and Canada. In Canada, it took one of the rare Marston trout which seldom fall for a fly, and it raised a fine salmon in England."*

*—Lew Oatman, "Shushan Postmaster,"* Esquire, *March 1956*

The Shushan Postmaster appears in two chapters of *The Founding Flies*—not the classic bucktail itself, but the man for whom Lew Oatman tied the fly. That man was Al Prindle, a colorful character who, from 1935–1947, was postmaster of the tiny community of Shushan, New York, on the banks of the Battenkill River. Oatman cherished the man, as did Lee Wulff, who said Prindle was "the most memorable of all my fishing companions." Illustrator Norman Rockwell, who at the time lived up the road in Arlington, Vermont, used Prindle as his model for his Four Seasons calendar art. It seemed the entire community loved the guy; it is no wonder Lew Oatman named a fly after him.

There are images of Lew and "the postmaster" in *The Founding Flies*, photos taken by the same photographer who contributed to Oatman's 1956 *Esquire* article that told the story of the beloved "Dean of the Battenkill River." In the laborious task of tracking down many people who had connections with "the founding flies" and their creators, I found Herb Eriksson, who knew Oatman and followed him around with his camera during the 1950s.

Herb, now 91 years young, allowed me to use his photographs for the book, great additions to the Oatman chapter. But the benefit of finding Herb went far beyond use of his pictures; we have

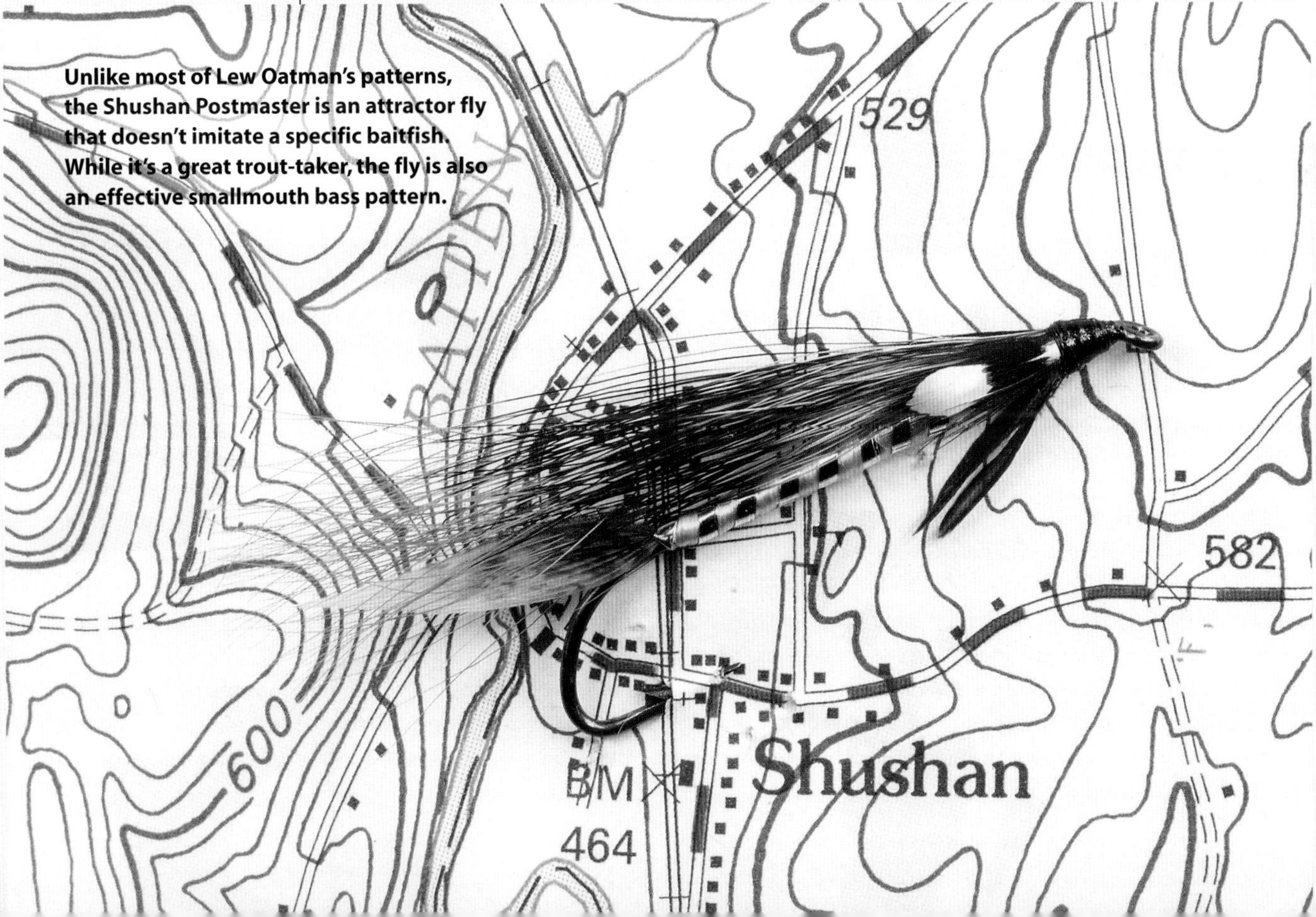


**Unlike most of Lew Oatman's patterns, the Shushan Postmaster is an attractor fly that doesn't imitate a specific baitfish. While it's a great trout-taker, the fly is also an effective smallmouth bass pattern.**

The Spring Hole, on the Battenkill River, Shushan, New York. During the 1950s, Lew Oatman tied flies in a home on Roberson Road, walking distance from the pool. The Spring Hole was named for the numerous springs that feed cold water into the pool. But it's also a great pool to fish in the spring of the year with streamer patterns.

since become good friends. We see each other frequently now, both at his home and studio but also on the banks of the Battenkill at Shushan. Herb frequently stops by my little fishing cabin in Shushan, just up the road from the Battenkill where Lew Oatman once lived along its bank and where he tied his streamers. Always with camera in hand, he shoots away if he finds me tying flies. It's rare to see Herb without a camera around his neck.

One day Herb was out for a drive with his wife Doris when he spotted my vehicle parked at Buffum's Bridge on the river and pulled over to chat. I had a question for him: "Do you remember where Lew Oatman and postmaster Al Prindle were fishing in that photo we used in the *The Founding Flies*?"

"I'll show you right now," was his response. We drove to a spot on the river a couple miles downstream. "There," he said as he pointed to a bend in the river. "It was right there, back in the mid-1950s. Lew and Al Prindle came up the riverbank. I told the two to hold it right there, and I snapped some photos of them, about right where we're standing now. I also have other photos of Prindle coming out of the river right here, too. Got one of him stepping through the barbed wire fence that used to run along this riverbank."

All fishing flies have a story attached to them—how they were named or other circumstances that led to their creation. The pattern featured here, The Shushan Postmaster, is no different.

## Fishing the Shushan Postmaster

Unlike most of Oatman's patterns, the Shushan Postmaster is an attractor fly that doesn't imitate a specific baitfish. While it's a great trout-taker, the fly is also an effective smallmouth bass pattern. My experience with bass fishing leads me to believe they'll take most any kind of fly you put in front of their nose, especially if it's colorful, and this pattern fits that description. However, my own experiences with the Shushan Postmaster are primarily on trout streams and large wilderness ponds. Brook trout love the fly, especially tied in smaller sizes, such as size 12. I love fishing the fly on brook trout tributaries flowing into the Battenkill River, such as Camden Creek.

It's a good pattern on small brooks, but also performs well for taking big brook trout in large ponds and lakes. I've fished larger Shushan Postmasters, tied in hook sizes 6-8, when on the remote wilderness ponds in the Adirondack Mountains in New York State.

# Tying the Shushan Postmaster

Tying the Shushan Postmaster is so easy I'd recommend it for inclusion in beginning fly-tying courses. Red squirrel tail hair is readily available, inexpensive, and is manageable when tying a tuft to the hook shank for the pattern's wing. I've listed the Mustad 3665A since that was Lew's favorite streamer hook model. However, use any streamer hook model that's your preferred choice.

## DRESSING

| | |
|---|---|
| **Hook:** | #4-12 Mustad 3665A |
| **Thread:** | Black 6/0 UNI-Thread |
| **Tail:** | Turkey quill slip |
| **Rib:** | Lagartun flat gold tinsel |
| **Body:** | Danville yellow floss, four-strand |
| **Throat:** | Dyed red duck or goose quill fibers |
| **Wing:** | Red squirrel tail |
| **Cheeks:** | Jungle cock eyes |

**1.** Tie in thread at the hook bend. Cut a small section from a mottled turkey quill feather. Secure the feather section to the hook shank with a few thread wraps at a point just above the hook bend. Oatman liked tails about the width of the hook gap. I like my tails, on most flies, just a tad longer.

This 18-inch wild brook trout slammed a Shushan Postmaster on a remote wilderness pond in the Adirondack Mountains of New York. Brook trout love the bright color combination of red and yellow. The flashy tinsel found on the pattern's body also attracts fish.

**2.** Attach a length of flat gold tinsel directly in front of the tail. Again my preference is metal tinsel rather than Mylar, but use what you're comfortable with.

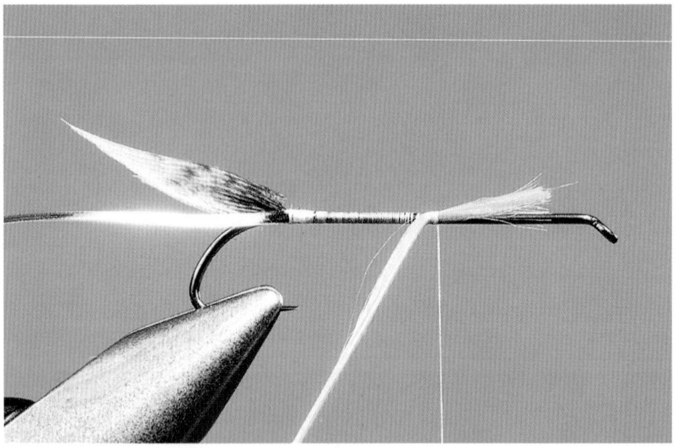

**3.** Wrap the thread over the tinsel and then to the midpoint of the hook shank, or a bit beyond that point. Attach a length of four-strand yellow floss.

**4.** Wrap the floss toward the hook eye, then secure with a couple thread wraps. Leave plenty of hook shank space to accommodate the remaining materials as well as the head.

**5.** Wrap the floss back down the hook shank to a point in front of the tail, then wrap back to the front. Secure the floss at the fly head area with a couple thread wraps. You'll end up with a slightly tapered body.

**6.** Grasp the gold tinsel and create the ribbing, with even winds, to the front of the fly.

**7.** Secure the tinsel with a couple of thread wraps, again being careful not to cut the thread if you're using metal tinsel. Snip off the excess tinsel.

**8.** Cut a slip from a dyed red duck or goose quill. The fibers will be used for the fly's throat.

**9.** Attach the red fibers underneath the hook at a point in front of the body. The fibers should be as long as the width of the hook gap, or just a bit longer. Tie off the white thread with a whip-finish knot, then tie on a piece of black thread for the remainder of the fly.

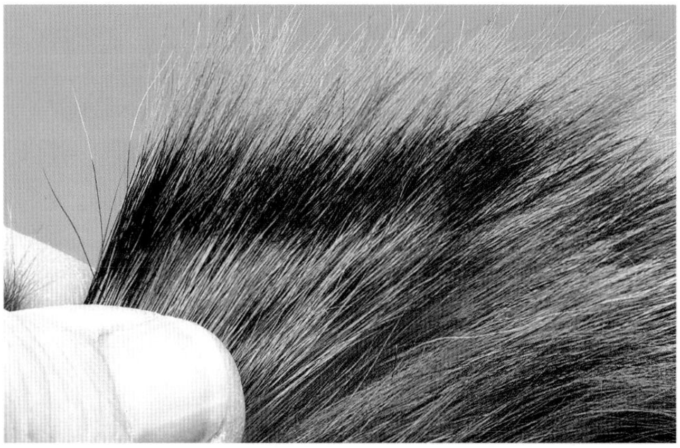

**10.** Cut a small amount of hair from a red squirrel tail to be used for the wing.

Squirrel tail hair has somewhat even tips but you can even them up even more, if you like, with a hair stacker.

**11.** Secure the squirrel tail hair, with a couple of black thread wraps, at the front of the body.

**12.** Snip off the remaining hair butts. Instead of chopping off the excess hair with a straight cut, place your scissors at an angle. It will be easier for you to create a nice tapered head.

**13.** Attach a small jungle cock eye, with a couple of thread wraps, to each side of the hook shank at the head position. Then clip off the excess.

**14.** Build the fly head with thread wraps then throw a whip-finish knot.

**15.** Add three coats of head cement, allowing each coat to dry thoroughly.

**16.** The completed Shushan Postmaster, the pattern created by Lew Oatman for his fishing friend Al Prindle.

Al Prindle, the Shushan Postmaster, crawling out of the Battenkill River in Shushan, New York. Herb Eriksson snapped the photo in the mid-1950s on a bend in the river directly behind what is now the Georgi Museum. The big tree is no longer there, but the river's beauty has not changed. HERB ERIKSSON

CHAPTER 18

# Usual

## *Dry fly*

*"When a fisherman observes him releasing a 16-inch brown on the Beaverkill or 20-inch rainbow on the Saranac and asks what pattern he's using, his answer is nearly always 'the usual.'"*

—*Fran Betters,* Fran Betters' Fly Fishing, Fly Tying and Pattern Guide, *1986*

The angler that Fran Betters, dean of New York's Ausable River, is referring to in that epigraph to the left is Bill Phillips. Phillips fished the tumbling Ausable since the 1930s and was an angling companion of Fran's father. He also fished with Ray Bergman and others in a "select group" of Ausable fly fishers, as Fran described them.

Bill Phillips's background as a chemistry and physics professor influenced how he evaluated the worth of trout flies. He looked at fly pattern design from the trout's perspective, how light refraction and a fly's translucency might affect a fly's potential as a fish-getter. A unique, unorthodox dry fly that Fran Betters was experimenting with caught Bill's quizzical attention one day when he stopped by Fran's fly shop, not far off the banks of the Ausable.

The bizarre dry fly was hackle-less, a simple tuft of fuzzy fur that looked like a wad of fluff from a clothes dryer lint trap. Beyond a fine-wire fishhook and some bright orange thread, its simple design required only one other material—fur from the pad of a snowshoe rabbit.

Fran was tying flies one day, and after pumping out quite a few, he decided to just do a little experimenting to break the monotony. He gazed around his tying table and noticed the snowshoe rabbit foot sitting on his table that he had put there months earlier after returning from a winter

**The Usual is an odd-looking trout fly with an odd name. Fran Betters, its creator, was fooling around one day at his tying vise when he grabbed the snowshoe rabbit foot sitting on his table. He noticed its qualities—its translucency, hair texture, and the fact that it was likely waterproof or water-resistant. The new dry fly became a hit throughout the country.**

West Branch of the Ausable River, in the Adirondack Mountains of New York, where Fran Betters fished many of his now famous patterns. The West Branch, a tumbling high-gradient river, will forever be known as Fran's River.

hunting trip. He grabbed it and noticed its qualities—its translucency, hair texture, and the fact that it was likely waterproof or water-resistant. Fran was well aware that snowshoe rabbits hop around on the snow for a good part of the year.

The new fly, without a name, emerged from Fran's tying vise. It looked "fishy" and worthy of his shop fly bin, so he tied a few more. Most customers were after Betters's Haystack and other patterns, and passed up the half-dozen new prototype dry flies. Soon after, though, Phillips walked in and took all six; they looked interesting and worth fishing. He had great success with the fly, and he never stopped fishing the pattern from that day forward. Bill routinely shared with other anglers that he was catching trout on "the usual fly." Fran decided to name it the Phillips Usual, more commonly abbreviated the Usual. The fly is an odd-looking pattern; some would have trouble recognizing it as an effective trout fly.

The Usual is now recognized and fished well outside of the Adirondacks and has colonized waters from East Coast to West Coast; it's been well received everywhere. The fly wasn't ignored in the Catskill region of New York, where shop bins were filled with elegant wood-duck wing dry flies. Walt and Winnie Dette and their daughter Mary—Catskill fly tiers in Roscoe, New York—eventually filled their shop bins with Usuals to meet requests for customers who came to fish the Beaverkill River and other historic area streams.

## Fishing The Usual

The Usual is a versatile pattern that can be floated over a rising fish or skittered across a riffle. It can be allowed to sink then teased into popping back up to the water surface by lifting the rod tip, mimicking an emerging nymph. The fly has a natural tendency to float. Yet as Fran noted in his *Fly Fishing, Fly Tying and Pattern Guide*, The Usual can be fished as a dry fly, wet fly, nymph, or emerging nymph. However, it's primarily fished as a floater.

## Tying the Usual

There are few effective trout patterns that are as easy to tie as the Usual. A frequent question arises concerning the pattern's primary material—fur from a snowshoe rabbit foot—and whether the fly can be tied with substitute materials. In his book, Fran wrote, "I'm sure any rabbit's foot would do as well, whether it be a cottontail or any one of the many domestic breeds."

Fran believed that the "steely color tones" found in the fur he preferred to use added to the pattern's attractiveness to fish, but suggested golden woodchuck underfur in the event a tier was unable to acquire a rabbit's foot. Fran sometimes mixed the golden underfur with the dark chocolate fur found next to the woodchuck's skin to tie darker Usual patterns. However, many fly-tying material supply houses have ample supplies of rabbit feet, so there's no reason to use woodchuck fur if your goal is to tie the Usual in its original form and shade.

### DRESSING

| | |
|---|---|
| **Hook:** | #12-22 Mustad 94840, 94842 |
| **Thread:** | Fluorescent Orange 6/0 UNI-Thread |
| **Tail:** | Hair from rabbit foot pad |
| **Wing:** | Hair from rabbit foot pad |
| **Body:** | Underfur from rabbit foot pad, gray blend with light tan |

**1.** Snip off a tuft of hair from the pad of a snowshoe rabbit footpad. Split the foot joints to access the soft fur and guard hairs you'll need to tie this simple pattern. All you have to do is stick a knife blade point or screwdriver between the joints and then twist the joints apart.

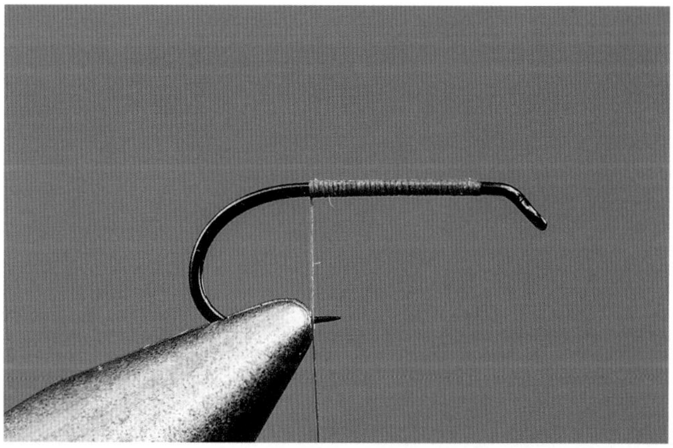

**2.** Start the hot-orange tying thread at the eye-end of the hook and then wrap down to the hook bend. The thread will then show through the body material, an effect that makes the fly attractive to fish—in theory. The hair, especially the wing, will also stay in place a bit better if it's bound down to a thread base rather than a bare hook shank.

**3.** Attach a clump of snowshoe footpad guard hairs at the hook bend area, then secure the tail with a couple thread-wraps. The excess hair is snipped off.

**4.** Wrap tying thread to a point about the middle of the hook shank, or slightly beyond that point.

**5.** Snip off a small amount of footpad guard hairs for the wing. Bind the tuft to the hook shank with two or three thread wraps.

**6.** Dam up the wing by winding several thread wraps close against the front of the hair. The wing should be upright a bit, but still at a slight forward attitude.

**7.** Wrap the tying thread over the wing hair butts and to a point back at the front of the hair tail. The thread is now positioned to accept the fur body dubbing.

Spin the soft, gray-shade snowshoe rabbit underfur on the thread using your method of choice. You can add a small coating of wax to the thread, to help keep the fur attached to the thread as you're creating the fly body.

**8.** Wrap the fur dubbing body forward to the wing base.

**9.** Pull back the wing with your thumb and index finger and then continue the dubbing wraps in front of the wing. You'll end up just short of the hook eye. Leave enough space for a small head. Notice that the hot-orange thread shows through the gray dubbing fur.

**10.** Throw a whip-finish knot at the head.

**11.** Add a drop of head cement.

**12.** The Usual is now complete. It's about as simple a fly as can be tied, but it can be as effective as the most difficult to tie dry-fly pattern you've ever fished.

The New York stretches of the Battenkill River provide great fall fishing. Brown trout readily strike many of the founding flies.

CHAPTER 19

# Western Coachman

## *Semi-dry fly*

*"I may be wrong in the value of this particular hair in fish appeal but to say that I have released 1700 trout in one season taken on this fly is a pretty fair yardstick."*

—*Buz Buszek, undated letter to book author and* Outdoor Life *fishing editor Ray Bergman, late 1940s or early 1950s.*

The Western Coachman is a spin-off pattern of the traditional Coachman wet fly, a classic pattern that nineteenth-century fly tier and author Mary Orvis Marbury called, in her *Favorite Flies and their Histories* (1892), "The most general favorite of any fly used in America." The traditional Coachman fly is credited to Tom Bosworth, who served as coachman to three members of the royal family—George IV, William IV, and Queen Victoria.

Modern fly fishers, such as the Joe Brooks, embraced the Coachman wet fly as a favorite pattern. Buz Buszek felt the same way about his own Western Coachman. The Buz Buszek chapter in *The Founding Flies* describes the story of Buz and his patterns, the Western Coachman among them as his signature fly.

Much of the information concerning the Western Coachman that appeared in *The Founding Flies* came from Buz himself, in an undated letter he had written to Ray Bergman. Jill and Mark Schwarz, from Nyack, New York, graciously allowed me access to files that held Ray Bergman's original correspondence. Nyack was Bergman's hometown; Jill inherited the letters that had belonged to Bergman's nephew, Buddy Christian.

**The Western Coachman, a pattern developed by Wayne "Buz" Buszek in the 1930s. It's not truly a wet fly but rather a "semi-dry fly." It's fished mostly slightly subsurface, somewhat like an emerging insect. Buszek once took 1,700 trout on the fly in one season.**

The Tule River, in California, is the birthplace of Buz Buszek's Western Coachman. DAVE JOHNSON

It was on a Saturday in September 2011 that Mark and Jill allowed me to rummage through Ray Bergman's documents and correspondence in preparation for crafting the Ray Bergman chapter in *The Founding Flies*. That's when I came across Buszek's unpublished letter concerning the history of the Western Coachman. Other information that gave insight into the Western Coachman's development was gathered from documents and taped interviews provided by my friend Dave Johnson of Visalia, California. But the Western Coachman's story in an unpublished letter written by Buz was an unexpected find.

A scan of the original letter, as well as a photo of an original Western Coachman tied by Buz, appear in the Buszek chapter in *The Founding Flies*. In the letter, we learn that the Western Coachman was field tested on the Tule River Reservation, in the Sierra Nevada of California. That happened a long time ago—in the 1930s. The rainbows hammered the fly and from that point forward it became one of Buz's favorites and the favorite of many anglers. The Western Coachman received its biggest boost in 1949 when it was used for promotional purposes. The Pacific Olive Company distributed more than 2,000 Western Coachman flies as a sales gimmick.

The pattern sold well and fished well. Any trout fly that can bring one angler 1,700 trout in a season I'd say is quite an effective fly. The Western Coachman's effectiveness might be attributed to its design, which in turn affects the way it fishes.

## Fishing the Western Coachman

Concerning the Western Coachman, Don Lieb, who tied flies for Buszek's shop in the 1960s (see page 64), explained to me that the fly is not truly a wet fly but rather a "semi-dry fly." It's fished slightly subsurface, somewhat like an emerging insect. The fly never sinks more than a couple of inches deep and remains visible if the correct hair is used. You can see the fish strike because it's not totally out of sight as it drifts along the current. The other advantage with fishing this style fly is that once the fly starts to drag, it doesn't cause a surface wake that will usually turn a wary fish away.

## Tying the Western Coachman

It's important to use coarse white deer body hair when tying the wing on the Western Coachman. During the time Buz was experimenting with tweaking the common Coachman and Royal Coachman flies, he tried calf tail hair and bucktail hair for the wing. Both bucktail hair and calf tail hair have fine texture; deer body hair is coarse and hollow. Using fine-textured hair would cause the fly to sink, while hollow deer hair would enable the fly to float near the surface.

The Western Coachman is being tied here on a heavier-wire hook—the Mustad 7957BX. Buz offered the pattern tied in dry-fly fashion—no doubt on light-wire hooks—but the semi-dry-fly version was the most popular. The pattern's effectiveness is changed if a heavier-wire hook isn't used. I've listed the 7957BX because it's a favorite of mine, but use your preferred model.

## DRESSING

| | |
|---|---|
| **Hook:** | #10-14 Mustad 7957BX |
| **Thread:** | Black 6/0 UNI-Thread |
| **Tail:** | Golden pheasant tippets |
| **Rib:** | Gold wire (fine) |
| **Body:** | Peacock herl |
| **Hackle:** | Coachman brown hen or webby rooster |
| **Wing:** | Northern whitetail deer flank hair |

**1.** Select a golden pheasant tippet feather. Snip off a few fibers that will be used for tailing.

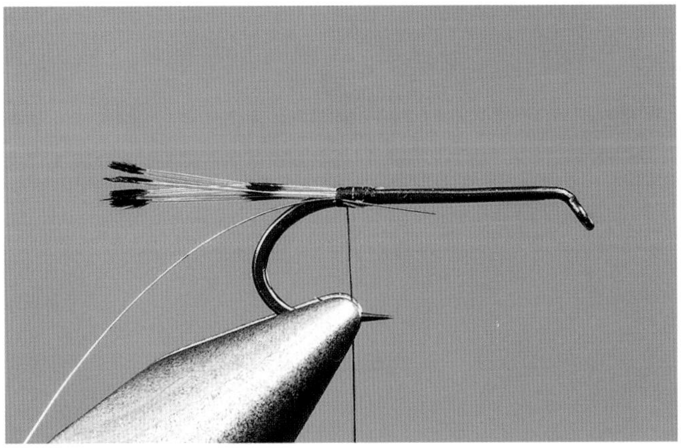

**2.** Tie in thread at hook bend. Tie in the golden pheasant tippets at the hook bend area along with a length of fine gold wire. The wire will add strength to the fragile peacock herl body.

**3.** Select one to two peacock herls, depending on hook size, from an area directly below the peacock eye. The thicker herls are found in that area of the peacock eye feather.

**4.** Attach the peacock herls directly in front of the tail.

**5.** Wind the first herl, if you're using two, to a point short of the hook eye, leaving plenty of room on the hook shank to accommodate the hackle and then the wing. Then wind the second herl over the first herl, to add more bulk to the body, if you're using a larger hook size. Don't crowd the hook eye.

**6.** Once both herls have been wound up the hook shank, grasp the gold wire and wind it forward, reinforcing the fragile herl. The wire is counter-wrapped through the herl (wrapped in the opposite direction of the herls).

**7.** End the gold wire directly in front of the peacock herl body. Secure with a couple thread wraps, then snip off the excess.

**8.** Select a webby, coachman brown hackle to be used for the fly collar. Use either hen hackle or soft, webby rooster hackle.

**9.** Attach the hackle, directly in front of the herl body, with a couple of thread wraps.

**10.** Wind the hackle forward with just a couple of turns.

**11.** Secure the last hackle wind with a couple of thread wraps, and then snip off the remaining excess hackle tip.

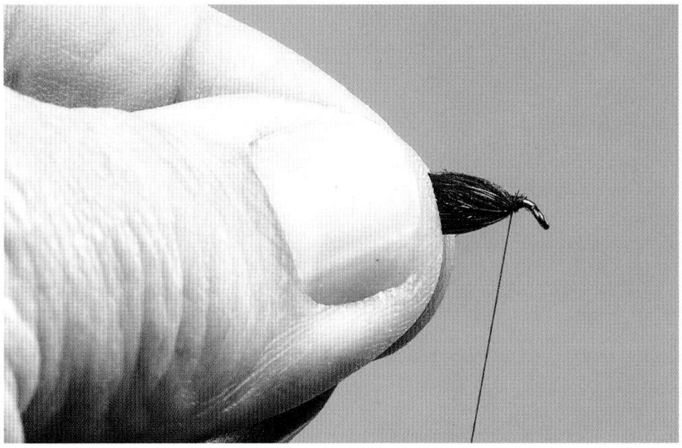

**12.** Pull back the hackle barb fibers, holding them with your thumb and index finger. Wrap thread around the front of the hackle to flare the fibers back.

**13.** With the hackle barbs flaring to the rear of the fly, you're now ready to attach the wing.

**14.** Stack a small tuft of northern whitetail deer flank hair. In the past, white rump or leg hair was also used for the wing.

**15.** Bind the small tuft of deer hair to the hook shank directly in front of the body. The hair should flare back to about the middle of the tail, or slightly longer. Snip off the remaining excess hair butts.

**16.** Throw a whip-finish knot and then form a head, making sure all the clipped hair butts are covered by thread.

**17.** Add a drop or two of head cement.

**18.** The Western Coachman, a pattern first created by Buz Buszek in the 1930s, is now completed.

CHAPTER 20

# Whitcraft

## *Dry fly*

*"The Adams and similar flies combining brown and Plymouth Rock [grizzly] will get my vote every time."*

—*Don Martinez, "The Right Dry-fly"* Field & Stream, *June 1953*

It would be rare to find a fly fisher who doesn't hold a high regard for the Adams, a pattern first crafted by Len Halladay of Mayfield, Michigan, in the early 1920s. In *The Founding Flies*, an entire chapter is devoted to Halladay and the story surrounding what is probably the most effective dry fly ever fished. It served as an archetype for many similar dry flies that followed.

Ever since the Adams was first cast on Mayfield Pond and the nearby Boardman River the pattern has been a favorite among fly anglers everywhere, regardless of location. The pattern has been tweaked into many variations—from parachute styles to enhanced creations such as Walt Dette's Delaware Adams. Don Martinez collaborated with Bob Carmichael near Jackson Hole, Wyoming, back in the 1940s and created the Whitcraft, a spin-off off the common Adams dry fly. The fly was named for Tom Whitcraft, a fishing superintendent who worked in Grand Teton National Park.

Martinez's chapter in *The Founding Flies* elaborates on the history of the Whitcraft, also called the Quill Adams, as well as other Martinez patterns. Those who are aware of Martinez and his fly-tying endeavors at West Yellowstone first associate him with the common Woolly Worm, a pattern he popularized. Yet he was a talented dry-fly man, credited by some for bringing the

**Don Martinez collaborated with Bob Carmichael near Jackson Hole, Wyoming, back in the 1940s to create the Whitcraft, a spin-off off the common Adams dry fly. The fly was named for Tom Whitcraft, a fishing superintendent who worked in Grand Teton National Park.**

Madison River, Yellowstone Park. Don Martinez fished many of his patterns on the Madison and other areas in Wyoming, Montana, and Idaho. He also sold patterns such as the Whitcraft, or Quill Adams, to fly anglers who came to the Madison in search of the fine trout that abound in its waters.

floater from the East Coast to Montana. His macaw quill body dry flies are some of his best creations; the Whitcraft is one of them.

## Fishing the Whitcraft

The Whitcraft will prove appropriate and worthy of your tippet on any occasion where you would fish an Adams dry fly. I haven't fished a Whitcraft in years—and even then it was a slightly different version from Martinez's original—but I intend to do so again this coming season. When I'm throwing out long loops with a Whitcraft on the delivery end, my thoughts will for certain turn to Martinez and the picturesque fishing surroundings he must have experienced during his years in Jackson Hole and West Yellowstone, times when he was tying great numbers of the fly. I had never visited Teton country near Jackson Hole until I was working on *The Founding Flies*, years after I first read about the Whitcraft and its story in J. Edson Leonard's book *Flies* (1960). My visit to what was once Don Martinez's world was nothing short of inspirational.

## Tying the Whitcraft

If you've already mastered the classic Adams dry fly, you'll find that the Whitcraft is an easy pattern to tie. The only difference between the two is the body material. The Adams is tied with muskrat or other gray dubbing while the Whitcraft is crafted with macaw quill. Don Martinez enjoyed tying dry-fly bodies and nymphs with macaw quill fibers, a material that provides interesting blue, gold and gray shades once wound on the hook shank. It's also fairly strong compared to other quill-like materials. Macaw wing quill is popular with salmon fly tiers, is readily available, and not too expensive, considering a number of flies can be tied with just one feather.

## DRESSING

**Hook:** #12-16 Mustad 94840
**Thread:** Tan 6/0 UNI-Thread
**Wing:** Grizzly hackle tips
**Tail:** Mixed brown and grizzly hackle barbs
**Body:** Yellow and blue macaw quill, or equivalent shade material
**Hackle:** Mixed brown and grizzly

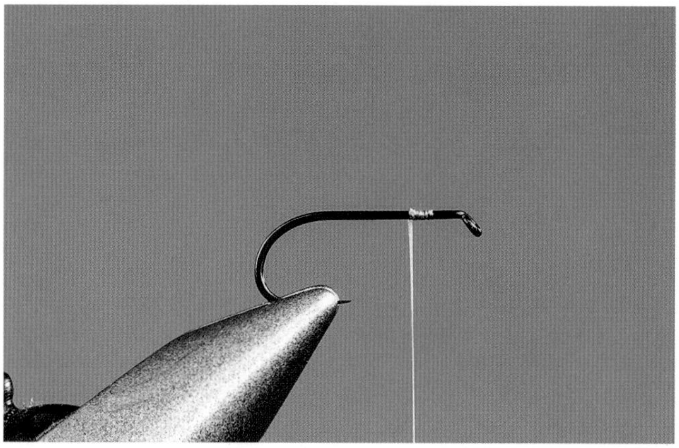

**1.** Start the thread at the two-thirds point on the hook shank.

**2.** Select two grizzly rooster hackles that have rounded points. You can also use hen hackle, but rooster was original with the pattern. I still prefer rooster hackle point wings on all my Adams dry flies and Adams spin-off patterns such as the Whitcraft.

**3.** Place the convex sides (shiny sides) of the two grizzly hackles against each other so that once tied on the hook shank, the wings will diverge. It's best not to cut out the hackle points from the entire feathers when attaching to the hook. You'll trim the long feather stem once the wings are secured to the hook shank. Some barbs should be left on the stem to reinforce the center quill. Hackle point wings can be fragile, and they need strength at their attachment points on the hook. Some barb fibers will flare out in the process of tying in, but you can trim the strays away.

**4.** Dam up the hackle point wings by making several thread wraps directly in front of the wing bases. The wings will then assume an upright attitude.

**5.** Make a couple more thread wraps around the wing bases to soundly position the wing. Also run the thread between the wings—rear to front and then front to rear—to separate the wings.

**6.** Select the largest brown and largest grizzly hackles that have long, stiff barbs for tailing.

**7.** Mix the two shades together and then tie in at a point on the shank above the hook point. The tails should be as long as the hook shank or even a little longer. I prefer long tails on my dry flies.

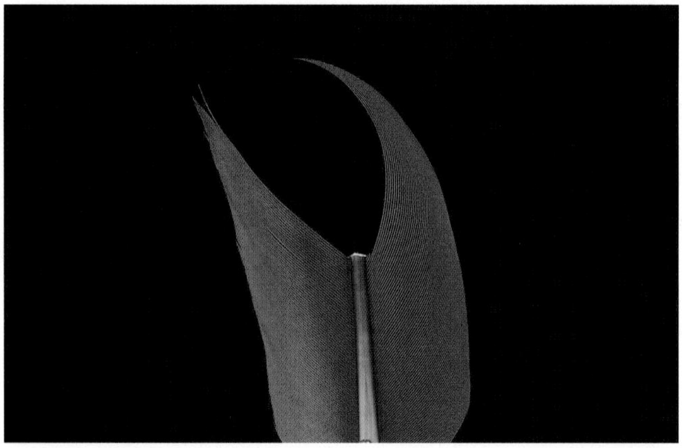

**8.** Select a macaw wing quill that has both mustard-yellow and dark blue shades. Macaw is readily available, but if you like, you can experiment with other quills that when dyed will give the same body shade—yellow and blue mixed.

**9.** Snip off three or four fibers from the macaw feather, depending on the hook size, and then attach at the tail position.

**10.** Grasp the macaw fibers with hackle pliers, and then wrap forward, twisting the fibers as you progress toward the base of the wings.

**11.** Snip off the remaining excess macaw fibers once you secure the ends with a couple thread wraps. The body will have a variegated shade of blues, yellows, and grays.

**12.** Select one grizzly hackle and one brown hackle, and then measure the barbs for the hook size you're using. The barbs should measure one and a half times the hook gap width.

**13.** Tie in both hackles at the wing base. Secure with a couple thread wraps.

**14.** Grasp the brown hackle and wind forward three turns in back of the wing and two turns in front.

**15.** It's best not to make the winds too tight next to each other. Leave a little space between each wrap for the grizzly hackle that will follow. Secure the brown hackle with a couple thread wraps. You can either snip off the excess brown hackle point now or later, at the same time that the excess grizzly hackle is snipped off once that feather is wound forward.

**16.** Use a slight weaving, back-and-forth motion as you wrap the grizzly hackle forward. The weaving will lessen the chance of matting down the brown hackle during wrapping. Secure the grizzly hackle just short of the hook eye with a couple thread wraps.

**17.** Snip off the excess grizzly hackle point, along with the excess brown hackle point if that hasn't been removed.

**18.** Add a drop of head cement.

**19.** The Whitcraft, or Quill Adams, is now completed. A great pattern that is still worthy of a fly-fisher's box.

# CHAPTER 21

# Woodruff

## *Dry fly*

*"The rise proved disappointing to everyone but Johnny, who took a basketful of handsome fish, six or seven of them, and made a great hit on his return to the clubhouse."*

*—Harold Smedley,* Fly Patterns and Their Origins, *1944*

The "Johnny" that Smedley is referring to in that quote to the left is Johnny Woodruff, who was fishing on the Brooklyn Fly Fishers Club waters on the upper Beaverkill River. As the story goes, in 1920 Chester Mills of the William Mills & Son tackle house in New York City handed Woodruff a small supply of a new fly and asked him to fish them. He showed club members the new fly, but it failed to impress them. A few members were inside the clubhouse eating dinner. Another member, who had still been on the stream fishing, rushed in and interrupted them. There was a terrific rise in progress on the stream. Everyone left the dinner table in a rush, flew out the door, grabbed their rods, and fished. Woodruff had the last laugh because he was the only one who took fish that evening—on a Woodruff. Because after a showing like that, Mills could hardly name the fly after anyone but Johnny.

John Woodruff was a Catskill-region fly shop hang-around during the early years that Walt and Winnie Dette started tying trout flies commercially. Walt loved to tell the story about how Woodruff would stop by the shop and would more than gladly accept an alcoholic beverage—or two, or three. It was hard to get rid of him, once he'd had a few. However, the Dettes once offered the Woodruff dry fly as one of their standard patterns and included it in their early 1930 catalog listing.

**The Woodruff is an old pattern field-tested and popularized in the 1920s by Brooklyn Fly Fishers Club member Johnny Woodruff, who found success with it on New York's Beaverkill River. It makes for a great caddisfly flutterer.**

Brown trout readily strike many of the founding dry flies. Among classics such as the Quill Gordon, Hendrickson, and Dark Coty is the Woodruff.

There's a photo in *The Founding Flies* of a 1930s-era Dette-tied Woodruff that Walt mounted in a shadow box decades ago. His daughter Mary insisted that I remove and photograph it, along with many other patterns, for the Dette chapter in the book. As might be assumed, any fly that was first crafted in 1920 probably underwent some changes over the years. The Woodruff was no different—there are a few variations, mostly in body shade.

## Fishing the Woodruff

In addition to being an effective attractor pattern, skipped over riffles, the Woodruff makes for a great fluttering caddis imitation. We have no way of knowing if Johnny Woodruff had encountered a caddis hatch during that evening on the Beaverkill back in the 1920s but it's plausible that's what happened. In those early years, before tiers paid much attention to imitating caddisflies, fly anglers turned to patterns that were not specifically intended as imitations for that particular insect. Anglers were fishing the Conover and other flies such as the Woodruff.

## Tying the Woodruff

Up until at least the 1930s, the Woodruff was tied with olive-shade wool—at least, that's what Walt and Winnie Dette used for their Woodruff body material. By the 1960s, Harry and Elsie Darbee, Catskill fly tiers who were once partners with the Dettes, were using a light chartreuse wool body shade on their Woodruffs. They also used ginger hackle barbs for tailing. As is true with many early patterns, dressings were changed and altered over time. Some versions are darker olive than others. Yellow or light chartreuse versions also exist, tied with wool or even floss. The pattern can be tied with wings in either a full-spent or semi-spent position. In the example that follows, I've selected a semi-spent wing attitude.

The Woodruff body was originally tied in the 1920s with olive wool. However, tiers over the years recognized that wool isn't the best body material to use in a dry fly. While it's difficult to remember for sure, in my early tying years I probably tied my Woodruffs with wool. Wool was, and still is, inexpensive and readily available. I abandoned wool as a primary body material on dry flies sometime back in the 1970s, preferring natural fur blends. The body material I'm using here is a dyed rabbit fur blend—a mix of dark olive, olive brown, and pale yellow.

As is the case with other hackle-point wing dry flies, you can also use hen hackle instead of grizzly. However, rooster was original with this pattern, as it was with many other classic dry flies. Rounded rooster hackle points were bred out with the advent of genetic hackle that replaced old barnyard-raised Plymouth Rock ("grizzly") chickens

## DRESSING

| | |
|---|---|
| **Hook:** | #12-16 Mustad 94840 |
| **Thread:** | Tan 6/0 or 8/0 UNI-Thread |
| **Wing:** | Grizzly hackle tips |
| **Tail:** | Grizzly hackle barbs |
| **Body:** | Hareline Dubbin rabbit fur, in a blend of dark olive, olive-brown, and pale yellow |
| **Hackle:** | Brown |

**1.** Select two grizzly rooster hackles that have rounded points.

**2.** Tie thread on hook at the two-thirds point on hook shank. Position the wing feathers convex side to convex side (shiny side of the hackle to shiny side of the hackle) so they will flare out when the hackle points are tied in on the hook shank. Secure with a couple thread wraps. Run tying thread up between your thumb and index finger and pull down, firmly securing the "pinched" feathers to the hook.

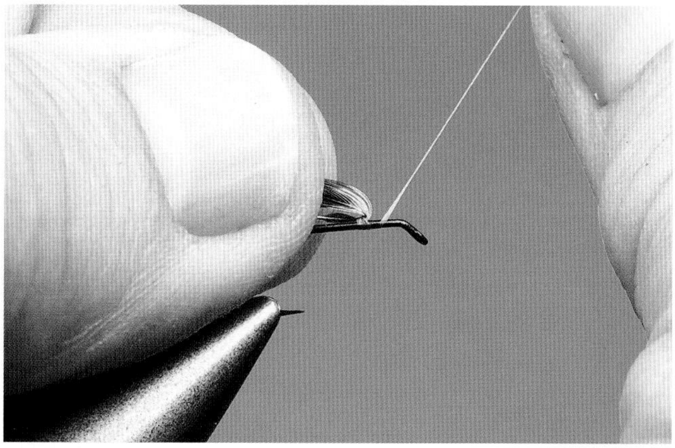

**3.** Hold the wings between your thumb and index finger and then pull the hackle points to the rear. Dam up the wings with a few thread wraps.

**4.** Divide wings by running tying thread between the upright wings—rear to front then front to rear. The wing attitude will end up as shown. The wing attitude should be spent or semi-spent, flaring out rather than assuming a more upright position.

**5.** Once the wings are positioned with a spent attitude, secure with several additional thread wraps between and around the wings.

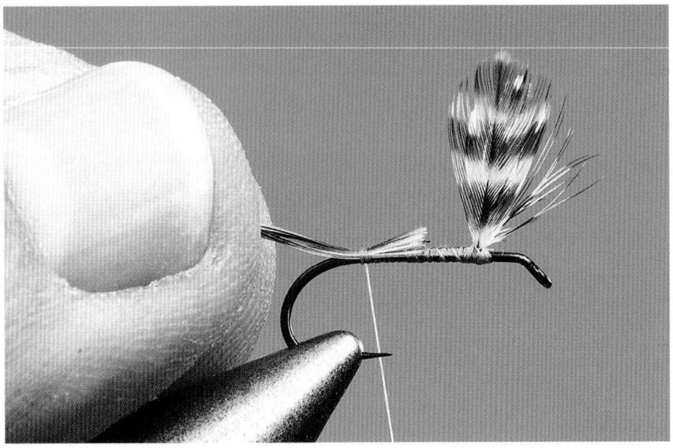

**6.** Select long, stiff grizzly rooster hackle barbs for tailing. Secure with a couple thread wraps at the hook bend area.

**7.** The tails should be about as long as the hook shank.

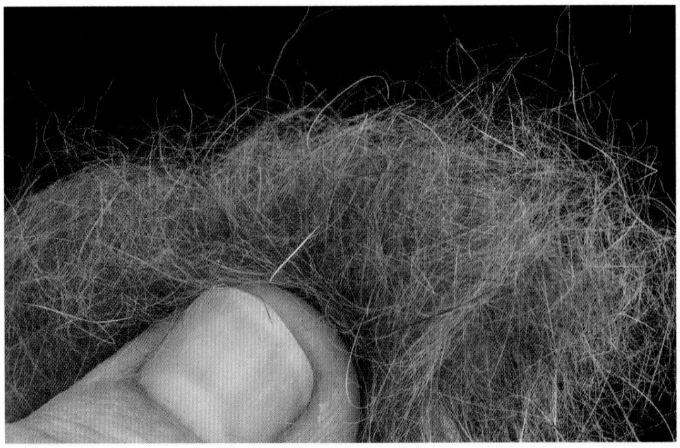

**8.** Create the rabbit fur dubbing blend: Hareline Dubbin dark olive shade is blended with olive brown shade, 50-50. Once that's blended, a small amount of Hareline Dubbin pale yellow shade is mixed in. Roughly, the blend is about 90 percent olive-brown/dark olive and 10 percent pale yellow.

**9.** Tease the blended dubbing into a spindle then attach to the hook shank at the tail. You can add dubbing to the thread using your own method or the spindle technique, as shown here. Raise the thread up into the dubbing rope and then twist together as a unit.

**10.** Wrap the body forward to a point just behind the wing bases.

**11.** Tie in the brown hackle at a point behind the wing. Since the Woodruff is a Catskill pattern, I've selected hackle with the barbs twice the hook gap width. However, you can choose hackle size to meet your own preference.

**12.** Wind the hackle forward with three wraps behind the wing and a couple of wraps in front of the wing.

**13.** Snip off any excess hackle, being careful not to snip your thread.

**14.** Finish the head with a whip-finish knot and then add a drop of head cement.

**15.** The completed Woodruff, an excellent pattern that floats and fishes well on most any stream. Try it in a variety of sizes.

# BIBLIOGRAPHY


Atherton, John. *The Fly and the Fish*. New York: Macmillan Co., 1951.

Bates, Joseph D., Jr. *Streamer Fly Tying and Fishing*. Harrisburg, PA: Stackpole Co., 1966.

Bergman, Ray. *Trout*. 1938; reprint, New York: Alfred A. Knopf, 1945, 1952.

———. *With Fly, Plug, and Bait*. New York: William Morrow & Co., 1947.

Betters, Fran. *Fran Betters' Fly Fishing, Fly Tying, and Pattern Guide*. 2nd ed. Wilmington, NY: Ausable Wulff Products, 1986.

Betters, Fran, Eric Leiser, and Warner Wales. "How Many Flies Can a Woodchuck . . ." *Fly Fisherman*. June 1978, 77, 87–88.

Brooks, Joe. "Best All-Round Trout Fly." *Outdoor Life*. October 1963: 64–65, 149, 151–157.

Camp, Raymond. *Noll Guide to Trout Flies*. Doylestown, PA: H.J. Noll Co., 1964.

Flick, Art. *Streamside Guide to Naturals and Their Imitations*. New York: G. P. Putnam's Sons, 1947.

Fox, Charles K. "A New Kind of Fly." *Fisherman*. March 1958: 24–25, 54–55.

Hofland, T. C. *The British Angler's Manual*. London: Whitehead and Co., 1839.

Leiser, Eric. *The Complete Book of Fly Tying*. New York: Alfred A. Knopf, 1977.

———. "Tying the Llama Fly and Why." *Fly Fisherman*. June/July 1973: 56–62.

Leonard, J. Edson. *Flies*. New York: A. S. Barnes and Company, 1960.

Lively, Chauncy. "The Carpenter Ant." In *Fishermen's Digest*, edited by Tom McNally. Chicago: The Gun Digest Company, 1964.

Marbury, Mary Orvis. *Favorite Flies and Their Histories*. 1892; reprint, Boston: Charles T. Branford Co., 1955.

Marinaro, Vincent C. *Modern Dry-Fly Code*. New York: G. P. Putnam's Sons, 1950.

Martinez, Don. "The Right Dry-fly." *Field and Stream*. 58. No. 2, June 1953: 68–72.

McClane, A. J., ed. *McClane's Standard Fishing Encyclopedia*. New York: Holt, Rinehart and Winston, 1965.

———. "One for the Book." *Field & Stream*. July 1951: 67.

———. *The Practical Fly Fisherman*. New York: Prentice-Hall, 1953.

———. "The Michigan Stone." *Pennsylvania Angler*. February 1971: 22–23.

Merwin, John. *The Battenkill*. New York: Lyons & Burford, Publishers, 1993.

Niemeyer, Ted. "The Caddis Explosion." *Fly Fisherman*. April 1977: 56.

Oatman, Lew. "The Shushan Postmaster." *Esquire*. March 1956.

———. "Streamer Flies From Nature's Patterns." *Esquire*. 46. No. 2, August 1956.

Puyans, André M. "Tying the A.P. Nymph Series." *Angler*. May/June 1975: 21–26.

Rosborough, E. H. "Polly." *Tying and Fishing the Fuzzy Nymphs*. 1965; reprint, Manchester, VT: Orvis Company, 1969.

Schaldach, William J. *Currents & Eddies*. New York: A. S. Barnes and Company, 1944.

Schwiebert, Ernest. *Remembrances of Rivers Past*. New York: Macmillan Co., 1972.

———. *Trout*. New York: E. P. Dutton, 1978.

Shenk, Ed. "Sublime to the Ridiculous: The Miniature Jassids." *Field & Stream*. June 1968: 52, 133–136.

Solomon, Larry, and Eric Leiser. *The Caddis and the Angler*. Harrisburg, PA: Stackpole Books, 1977.

Smedley, Harold Hinsdill. *Fly Patterns and Their Origins*. 2nd ed. North Muskegon, MI: Forsyth Press, 1944.

Valla, Mike. "Chauncy K. Lively (1919-2000)." *Eastern Fly Fishing*. Winter 2012: 76–79.

———. *Founding Flies*. Mechanicsburg, PA: Stackpole Books, 2013.

———. "Highway 20 Corridor, NY: Beating the Heat in the Summer." *Eastern Fly Fishing*. July/August 2011: 36–41.

———. *Tying Catskill-Style Dry Flies*. New Cumberland, PA: Headwater Books, 2009.

# INDEX

Page numbers in italics indicate photographs or illustrations.